BEYOND ASIAN AMERICAN POVERTY

Community Economic Development Policies and Strategies

Project Director

Paul Ong

Research Team

Dennis Arguelles
Susan Castro
Bruce Chow
Chanchanit Hirunpidok
Tarry Hum
Winnie Louie
Erich Nakano
Paul Ong
Roderick Ramos

LEAP Asian Pacific American
Public Policy Institute

BEYOND ASIAN AMERICAN POVERTY

Community Economic Development Policies and Strategies

To our parents,
whose struggles embody the spirit and purpose
of this book

Leadership Education for Asian Pacifics (LEAP)
327 East Second Street, Suite 226
Los Angeles, CA 90012-4210

Printed in the United States of America.

Cover photo: Song Yon Cho
Cover design: Paula Sherman

CONTENTS

ACKNOWLEDGEMENTS

This book would not have been possible without the support of several individuals and organizations. We are grateful to the Asian Pacific American Public Policy Institute of the Leadership Education for Asian Pacifics (LEAP) and the Asian Pacific Planning Council (APPCON) for sponsoring this project and providing valuable guidance throughout its development. LEAP and the ARCO Foundation provided partial funding for the research and publication of this book, and UCLA's Urban Planning Program and Asian American Studies Center provided technical support and guidance. Some of the concepts presented in this book were initially developed through a project supported by PRRAC (Poverty and Race Research Action Council). We are indebted to Glen Omatsu and Mark Garrett for helping prepare the final manuscript. We are grateful to the following students who helped us conduct the Survey of Asians in Low Income Communities (SALIC), which included over 300 households:

Edna Baradas
Linda Chau
Maisie Chin
Dennis Garcia
Carmela Gonzales
Xuan Han
Dong Hoang
Molly Huynh
Alyssa Kang
Maryanne Kim
Laphone Louplor
Huy Quoc Luu
Bory Yasmin Ouk
Peter Park
Julie Silva
Sylvia Tam
Took Took Thongthiraj
Khai Tran
Vickie Wang
Jodi Yamamura

Several other individuals should be acknowledged for giving time, guidance and assistance to this project, including J.D. Hokoyama, Executive Director of LEAP, and Linda Akutagawa, Office Manager. Many thanks to Deborah Ching, APPCON President and Executive Director of the Chinatown Service Center. Countless other individuals who we cannot name here also deserve much thanks and appreciation for their support.

Although we received valuable input from numerous individuals, we alone are responsible for the contents of this book.

This book is the product of a year-long comprehensive project by researchers at UCLA's Urban Planning Program. We set out to provide community leaders and policy-makers much needed information on the economic needs of Asian Americans, and to formulate a framework for Community Economic Development (CED) in Asian American communities. We want this book to be more than just another policy or academic report. Our intent is to help empower Los Angeles' "invisible" Asian population, the over 124,000 who are part of the working poor, the unemployed or those dependent on welfare. The existence of this segment of the population dispels the "Model Minority" stereotype, which depicts Asians as having no economic needs or problems; nonetheless, community advocacy often focuses on middle-class and professional issues--- the "glass ceilings," the procurement of government contracts and college admissions.

This book focuses on the specific needs of the poor and provides recommendations for public policy and community action. We hope to enlighten the discussion of the role of Asian American communities in urban revitalization and the "rebuilding" of Los Angeles by challenging some existing approaches to economic development. This book is just the beginning of a long-term plan to organize and empower low-income Asian communities through CED. For us, theory and practice must go hand-in-hand. As a group and as individuals, most of the researchers have been working to implement the recommendations in this book.

BEYOND ASIAN AMERICAN POVERTY

EXECUTIVE SUMMARY

The following is a summary of research findings and policy recommendations from a year-long study on Community Economic Development (CED) in low-income Asian communities in Los Angeles. The study was conducted by a research group at the UCLA Urban Planning Program and sponsored by Leadership Education for Asian Pacifics (LEAP), the Asian American Public Policy Institute (AAPPI) and the Asian Pacific Planning Council (APPCON). The findings are based on an examination of census and other data sources, a Survey of Asian Low-Income Communities (SALIC) and a review of current federal, state and local economic development policies and programs.

Community Economic Development for Asian Americans

Global economic restructuring, capital flight and cuts in federal defense spending have created an economic and political crisis in Los Angeles. While a wide range of national and local policies and strategies are needed, Community Economic Development (CED) can play a significant role in improving conditions in local communities and neighborhoods.

CED can effectively address the economic needs of low-income Asian communities if it is adapted to their ethnic-specific characteristics. These communities have a large number of newer immigrants and refugees, extensive enclave economies, and a low-income population that is a part of the working poor. While traditional

CED strategies focus on small business development, an Asian strategy should incorporate efforts to improve Employment, Housing, Internal Capacity Building and External Political Linkages as well.

An effective CED strategy should target and involve the most disadvantaged members of a community. It should empower local residents, workers and merchants and provide them the necessary skills and resource to control the development of their community.

PART I ASIAN AMERICANS IN LOS ANGELES

Asians Living on the Margin/Inner-City Communities

Over 124,000 Asian Americans live in poverty in Los Angeles County, representing 13 percent of the Asian population. Almost 18,000, including many Cambodians and other Southeast Asians, are on welfare and face poverty rates as high as 45 percent. Many other Asians live above poverty but can not make a living wage.

A significant portion of low-income Asian Americans are at risk of being trapped in poverty. They will face poverty because they lack job skills and English language proficiency; their jobs offer few opportunities for advancement, and economic restructuring will continue to reduce the number of better-paying jobs in the labor market.

The concentration of Asians and other immigrants in ethnic enclaves such as Chinatown/Lincoln Heights, Koreatown/Filipinotown and Long Beach intensifies competition for low-wage jobs and affordable housing. But these geographic concentrations also offer opportunities to organize ethnic communities and develop a common agenda to improve living conditions.

Entrepreneurship and Enclave Economy

The majority of Asian small businesses are in the ethnic enclave economy, where access to a cheap immigrant labor force and an ethnically defined market are readily available.

The enclave economy is based on labor-intensive industries and concentrated in highly competitive sectors, where profits are marginal, wages low, workers benefits usually non-existent, and employment highly unstable.

The enclave economy serves as a crucial source of employment for immigrant workers who would be locked out of mainstream employment opportunities. But it is also a source of harsh and exploitative working conditions.

PART II RETHINKING POLICIES AND PROGRAMS

Job Training and Workers' Rights

Most low-income Asians are part of the working poor. Many of these individuals work full-time and year-round, but are still poor. They often lack transferable/marketable skills, English proficiency and knowledge of labor laws and job training opportunities and transportation. Moreover, their working conditions are often deplorable, unhealthy and unsafe. Among the jobless, those on public assistance face innumerable barriers to adequate employment.

Job training programs must be redefined so that they serve the most needy individuals. Current programs encourage "creaming," or the targeting of services to the most marketable applicants. Funding for job training and incentives to hire the disadvantaged must be increased. The application procedures for job training programs must be simplified and eligibility requirements relaxed since many immigrant workers cannot produce adequate documentation, which includes income information from the previous six months. Additionally, welfare policies should not penalize the poor, but provide more support and incentives to help them obtain employment. This should include larger refunds through the Earned Income Tax Credit to support the working poor.

The institutional framework to protect workers must be rebuilt. Government can support the right of workers to organize, and regulate the work environment to eliminate sweatshop conditions and other exploitative employer practices.

Alternative Business Development

Establishing small businesses and access to start-up capital are less significant for Asians as compared to other low-income minority communities, because entrepreneurship in Asian communities has been historically high. Instead, business development policies/strategies should address the large number of small enterprises that operate on the margins of profitability.

Programs should enhance the viability of existing businesses, rather than encourage new ones. Technical assistance is needed to help diversify these businesses. Additionally, the welfare of workers needs to be improved through health-insurance purchasing groups. Asian business owners should receive training on social responsibility to respond with cultural sensitivity to their employees and the communities in which they operate.

Policy-makers need to address Asian business development needs by 1) better linking immigrant enterprises with the greater Los Angeles/U.S. economy, 2) identifying and supporting economic growth areas, and 3) addressing loopholes in labor laws.

Affordable Housing

Housing is a fundamental need essential to individual and community well-being. Affordable housing, together with quality employment opportunities, can contribute to building economically and socially vibrant communities.

An affordable housing crisis exists in Los Angeles and affects a large number of poor Asians. An overwhelming majority of low-income households pay more than 30 percent of their income on rent, exceeding federal affordability guidelines.

The goal for Asian communities should be to increase the availability of quality and affordable housing through advocacy on various national and local housing policies. Additionally, Asians need to improve their ability to build affordable housing and other community facilities by establishing Community Development Corporations (CDCs).

PART III INSTITUTION BUILDING

Internal Organizational Capacity

Many Asian communities currently lack the organizational capacity to carry out CED work. Few resources are available to train staff and help Asian community-based organizations move into this field. Further, the training and funding that exist often exclude Asians because of mainstream perceptions that Asian communities have no economic problems.

Low-income residents must have a meaningful role in shaping economic development, identifying needs and developing strategies. Governmental advisory bodies such as redevelopment project area committees (PACs) have generally excluded low-income residents and Asian CBOs have few mechanisms to ensure their participation in policy/planning.

Capacity building and establishing Community Development Corporations (CDCs) should be the first priority in Asian communities. This can be carried out by expanding the role of existing CBOs or creating new institutions.

External Political Linkages

CED alone cannot solve the problems facing Asian communities. Community-based efforts must be complemented by advocacy and external political linkages. These linkages will enable Asian communities to influence policy- makers, government agencies, private foundations and other institutions.

Asians have much to contribute to inner-city economic development and should be partners in any urban revitalization strategy through coalitions with other racial/ethnic communities.

CHAPTER ONE

Community Economic Development for Asian Americans

Once the site of unmatched economic growth and opportunity and heralded for its multicultural diversity, Los Angeles is now in the midst of a political-economic crisis. Global economic restructuring and capital flight have led to the closing of heavy manufacturing plants, once the backbone of the region's economy, and their relocation to other states and the Third World. Selective deindustrialization has been further accelerated by the cuts in federal defense spending, which have devastated the region's once proud and highly profitable aerospace industry. As the victim of disinvestment, deteriorating infrastructure and governmental neglect, the inner city has endured the brunt of these changes, with poverty, unemployment and homelessness rates rivaling those in the Third World.

This economic decline has occurred during a period of increased immigration, including the arrival of low-skilled workers and political refugees from Asia. These people play an important role in the local economy by supplying labor for the growing sectors in retailing, light manufacturing and service industries. These immigrants are part of the working poor, or those who are unable to escape poverty despite full time and year-round employment. This dilemma is the primary issue facing low-income Asian communities in Los Angeles.

The solution to this political-economic crisis is not a moratorium on legal immigration, as suggested by the xenophobic Orange County Grand Jury which conveniently confuses the impact of illegal and legal aliens. The overwhelming majority of Asian immigrants are in this country legally. Their presence is testimony to the passage of the 1965 Immigration Act, and the solution must be finding ways to ensure that all Asian immigrants have the opportunities to become productive members of our society. This is in keeping with this country's historical commitment to being a nation of many people.

The civil unrest in the Spring of 1992 brought much attention to economic problems in Los Angeles and demonstrated the need for immediate and comprehensive social action. Policy-makers, academics, community activists, advocates and service providers have attempted to respond to this crisis with various strategies, the most visible of these being "Rebuild LA" (RLA). On a more local scale, one strategy that holds great potential is Community Economic Development (CED). CED is generally defined as the process by which a community increases, controls and organizes its resources so it can channel them toward its greatest needs. It focuses economic development efforts on the neighborhood and on the particular needs of a community.

However, the particular needs of low-income Asian communities require a unique approach to CED. These communities require a strategy that effectively deals with immediate employment, small business and housing needs but which also fosters political empowerment and recognizes the responsibilities associated with being members of a larger, multicultural and ethnically diverse society. Thus, we refine this general definition of CED to develop a model that addresses the specific needs of these communities. However, before discussing this CED model, it is necessary to understand how we define economic development, what makes our CED approach different from other approaches and why we feel it is an appropriate strategy for low-income Asian communities.

Development vs. Growth

We view economic development as a process of increasing a society's overall wealth as well as ensuring its equitable distribution. This means all society's members, particularly low-income and working sectors, receive tangible benefits from expanded economic activity. These benefits may include better housing conditions, higher wages, more meaningful employment opportunities, quality education and health care or other gains that do not always "trickle down" to whole communities.

This is different from general economic growth, which traditional economists associate with Gross National Product (GNP), increased productivity, higher profits and rising real estate values. These indicators do not guarantee that all members of society reap benefits. In fact, the 1980s saw record economic growth and profits under corporate restructuring and the policies of conservative administrations, while at the same time, an increase of those living in poverty. This transformation is probably best described in *The Great U-Turn*:

> Profits rebounded indeed, but the costs to American society have been--and continue to be--enormous. These public and private policies have led to a great U-turn in the American standard of living. After improving steadily for a generation, average wages have fallen, family incomes have stagnated, and wages, incomes and wealth have become increasingly polarized (Harrison and Bluestone, 1988, p. viii).

Between 1980 and 1990, the increase in the income of the richest one percent of Americans equaled that of the total income of the bottom 20 percent (Greenstein and Barancik, 1990, pp. 8-9). For Los Angeles in the same period, the disparity between the "have" and "have nots" increased more rapidly than for the U.S. as a whole (Ong et al., 1989).

Given the gross lack of "trickle down" from economic growth, the principle of fairness requires strategies that directly benefit those who are particularly disadvantaged. Traditional approaches to economic development for low-income populations have focused on business development and capital investment. While such activities are crucial, we view economic development as encompassing broader strategies that target and involve the working poor, unemployed, welfare dependent and others for whom small business development may not be a viable option.

The Role of Community in Economic Development

The concept of a "community" is difficult to operationalize because it means different things to different people. For the purpose of this book, we define community as a geographic area smaller than most cities but larger than a neighborhood block or census tract. The factors distinguishing a community are common social characteristics such as ethnicity, language or the existence of commonly shared cultural and religious institutions. Concentrations of ethnic small businesses and economic characteristics provide another identifier of a community.

Although economic development can be implemented at the regional, county, or city level, we believe that economic development must also be implemented at the community level. This is particularly true for low-income communities. Too often these areas are viewed as "ghettoes" and "slums" beyond repair. For those individuals who achieve some success, upward mobility means outward mobility, an exodus that saps the community of valuable human resources. Those less fortunate are trapped in deteriorating neighborhoods that become increasingly isolated from the rest of society. The goal of CED is to reverse this process. Though strategic long-term investment and development, residents can have decent and enjoyable places to live and meaningful employment opportunities. This not only help those who would otherwise be trapped in poverty, but it also gives upwardly mobile residents the option of remaining rather than having to move out to access better jobs and housing.

It is at the community level that economic development strategies are often most effective. Communities have well-developed social networks, organizations and cultural/religious institutions. These institutions create avenues through which large numbers of disadvantaged people can be reached and where, to some degree, they are already organized. This makes service delivery and other work associated with CED easier and more effective.

It is important to understand that Community Economic Development is one of many strategies which seek to address poverty and unemployment. Other strategies include relocating low-income people from areas of concentrated poverty, usually the inner-city, to areas where they are better absorbed by the local economy. This often manifests itself through the building of affordable housing in more affluent suburbs or through the resettlement of people to other states. These approaches are not in conflict with CED strategies.

Community Economic Development Principles

CED must be approached strategically and comprehensively. We feel that the complexity of the problems facing low-income communities requires a multi-faceted strategy which recognizes the need for broad economic and political change. Thus, rather than just attacking social problems such as juvenile delinquency, substance abuse and domestic violence, CED seeks to address the roots of these problems through the integration of service delivery with "bricks and mortar" development, community organizing and political empowerment.

This approach means identifying and prioritizing the community's most pressing needs, which we do in the first part of this book. This should be an on-going process, as the specific needs of a community are seldom static, but are affected by changes in immigration patterns, the local economy and housing market and are impacted by a community's cultural, religious and political institutions.

Next, CED work should be done by residents in low-income communities. This departs from traditional service-oriented approaches because in addition to providing needed services and facilities, the ultimate goal of CED is to organize these communities so that they can control and conduct their own development. However, CED differs from some traditional self-help strategies because it calls for greater government and private sector responsibility and attempts to empower low-income communities so that they can have an impact on public policy.

Of course, Community Economic Development cannot be a panacea for impoverished communities. CED has limitations primarily because it is a community-based approach to what are larger structural problems in the region's and nation's economy, particularly in this period of recession, capital flight and global economic restructuring. Thus, it is equally important for those using a CED strategy to complement their work with advocacy and organizing to promote changes in the larger society. CED can have significant impacts if it follows these principles, which are closely related to the building of institutions that provide a voice for the disadvantaged and the resources to carry out service provision, development work and organizing.

There are examples of how Community Economic Development can be implemented. Los Angeles' network of Community Development Corporations (CDCs) have over two decades of experience in this area. Among these is the Drew Economic Development Corporation, an extension of the Martin Luther King Hospital/Drew Medical School in the Watts/Willowbrook community. Drew EDC has developed several affordable housing projects and a child care center. It also provides small business development training and assistance to local residents.

Two of the oldest and largest CDCs in Los Angeles are The East Los Angeles Community Union (TELACU) and the Watts Labor Community Action Committee (WLCAC). Founded in 1965, these institutions have developed hundreds of affordable housing units, industrial parks and shopping centers and community/recreational facilities. They also operate job creation and training programs, often employing homeless and other unemployed individuals.

These types of institutions are greatly needed in Los Angeles' Asian community, yet only a few fledgling organizations have the capacity to carry out this type of work. Thus, the building and expansion of Asian CDCs are an integral part of our CED model.

Unique Features of Asian Communities

Community Economic Development holds much promise for low-income Asian communities, if it is approached strategically, comprehensively and involves, organizes and empowers the most disadvantaged members of the community. Asian American CED advocates can learn from existing strategies rather than reinventing the wheel. Other communities of color face similar sets of problems: poor employment opportunities, substandard housing and governmental neglect. However, CED efforts for Asian communities should not simply replicate those operating in African American and Latino neighborhoods. As we argue above, CED strategies must be responsive to the specific needs of each population. Low-income Asian communities have unique characteristics that require major modifications in CED approaches.

Among the unique characteristics of Asian communities are the large numbers of newer immigrants and refugees who, besides being poor, face a multitude of cultural and linguistic barriers. The problem is even more complex because low-income Asians are a culturally diverse population that does not share a common history, language, or social and religious institutions.

Another important feature is that many Asian communities have sizeable ethnic economies; thus they do not face the problem of disinvestment that adversely affects other minority communities. Self-employment and entrepreneurship rates are very high in most Asian communities. Consequently, the traditional approach of CED of increasing the level of economic activity through investment for new businesses is less relevant for Asian communities.

However, the Asian subeconomy is not without its problems. Many of the businesses are micro-sized "mom and pop"-type enterprises with marginal profitability. The employment that these small businesses create are often low-wage jobs with few benefits. Thus, critical issues center on the quality of jobs available and the viability of existing businesses, rather than generating new economic activity for the area.

Finally, Asians do not live or work in racially homogenous communities. Those residing in the inner-city live along side low-income Latinos, African Americans and whites -- a factor which needs to be considered in organizing and advocacy work. Moreover, many Asian small businesses operate in other low-income communities, and they are often embroiled in inter-ethnic conflict, as illustrated by tensions between Korean merchants and African American residents in South Central L.A.

A CED Model for Low-Income Asian Communities

Our model of Community Economic Development has five components:

1. Employment
2. Small Business Development/Improvement
3. Housing
4. Internal Capacity Building
5. External Political Linkages

The first three components of this model are "goals" of CED, or areas of work where concrete improvements can be gained in people's lives. The last two components are tools communities can use to carry out the work needed to achieve these gains.

Creating and improving employment opportunities in disadvantaged communities are fundamental elements of any CED strategy. This means providing opportunities so people can access jobs with decent wages, work in safe and secure environments and enjoy health benefits and chances for advancement.

These goals can be achieved by focusing efforts on job training and education to help workers gain higher paying jobs, as well as improving work conditions and pay for those at the lower end of the job market. In the area of job training, our focus is on the effectiveness of various government programs, with special attention given to English as a Second Language (ESL) programs. Of course, job training without the availability of jobs is of little use, so we also examine advocacy in the areas of job creation and economic development policy (which is discussed in Chapter Nine: External Political Linkages).

Additionally, our examination of various Asian community organizations indicates that the most organized and empowered sectors of the community tend to be professionals and business persons. As a result, most discussions about employment focus on the "glass ceiling" or the ability of Asians to move into upper management and administrative positions. In contrast, our concern is with raising the "floor." More attention needs to be given to the equally pressing needs of the working poor, who are concerned with issues such as minimum wage, workers benefits and workplace safety.

As stated earlier, small business development should be viewed as just one of a broad range of strategies aimed at improving conditions in low-income Asian communities. Given the existence of ethnic subeconomies with a relatively large number of existing firms, policies and programs should not focus on the creation of new businesses. Instead, the focus should be on improving existing businesses and diversifying the economic base. This means: 1) securing their long-term viability and competitiveness; 2) addressing the needs of workers in these businesses; and 3) promoting social responsibility among Asian business owners toward both their employees and the communities in which they operate.

Housing has long been recognized as a fundamental element in the well-being of a community. In low-income Asian communities, the lack of quality and affordable housing compounds already harsh economic conditions. Without adequate housing, residents are unable stabilize their lives and focus on school, employment and social relationships. Thus, improving housing conditions must be part of any overall CED strategy.

While housing for all income levels should be developed, our focus is on affordable housing, as this appears to be the greatest need. This includes increasing the housing stock by preserving and improving existing stock, advocating for long-term affordability and ownership programs and increasing tenant involvement and organization.

Carrying out the service delivery, development work, advocacy and organizing needed to truly improve conditions in the Asian community requires expanding existing and creating new community-based organizations. As discussed earlier, development work is a relatively new phenomena in Asian communities in comparison to other communities. Likewise, organizing and advocacy work which specifically targets Asian workers, tenants, immigrants and other disadvantaged sectors is not well developed. Thus, Chapter Eight of this book examines how such institutions and "capacities" can be built to meet these needs, including how community development corporations can play a role.

Finally, a CED strategy needs to recognize that the future of LA's Asian American community is inextricably tied to its ability to impact political institutions (city councils, government agencies, individual policy-makers, etc.) and to build linkages with other communities of color. Having an impact means pursuing traditional electoral work, fighting for better representation and holding elected officials accountable. It also requires forming coalitions and alliances with other ethnic communities. However, building coalition and improving inter-ethnic relations should not be viewed simply strategies; they are responsibilities that Asians have as part of a multiethnic society. Chapter Nine discusses the process of building these linkages, and presents a policy framework to guide community advocacy efforts.

Organization of this Book and Explanation of Methodology

This book is organized into three parts. The three chapters in Part I document the needs and conditions of Asians in low-income communities and the ethnic enclave economy, including political refugees and the working poor. We found that substantial numbers of Asians lack English fluency and job skills and access to culturally sensitive services. As a result, many are locked in poverty. Part II examines the three substantial areas of CED: business development, employment, and housing. The chapters provide an analysis of existing policies and programs, along with recommendations for both public policy and community action. Part III examines the tools needed to carry out CED work. These tools include the organizational capacity of Asian community-based organizations and the need for external political linkages. Finally, the book ends by outlining the steps to turn this CED strategy into action.

The data for our analysis comes from various sources. The needs assesment is based on four sources: 1) a Survey of Asians in Low Income Communities (SALIC), conducted by UCLA students in early 1993, which included over 300 face-to-face interviews with low-income households; 2) the 1990 U.S. Census Summary Tape Files (STFs); 3) a 5 percent sampling of resident characteristics from the Public Use Micro Sample (PUMS); and 4) a Survey of Minority-Owned businesses conducted by the U.S. Department of Commerce.

SALIC covered three geographic areas in Los Angeles. These areas not only met our definition of community, but were the sites of high concentrations of low-income Asians. The three communities which we identified are Chinatown/Echo Park/Lincoln Heights, Koreatown/Westlake and South Long Beach. An appendix on SALIC is included.

The PUMS data describes Asian residents living in the City of Los Angeles and the City of Long Beach. Unless otherwise specified, "Los Angeles" and "Long Beach" refer to those cities.

The analysis of policies and programs is based on a review of laws and programs, secondary material from published literature, and interviews with community leaders and program personnel.

PART I

ASIAN AMERICANS IN LOS ANGELES

Chapter Two

Asians Living on the Margin

I thought that if one has skills, experience and motivation to work, and if he puts his time and effort into his work, there would surely be some kind of reward in America. I believed that if I worked diligently, I could make it here. But I'm beginning to see that maybe it was all wishful thinking on my part. But I have not yet given up hope. God has guided us through the time in the past faithfully, and He will do so in the future.

Father of a recent immigrant family in Koreatown

There are countless Asian immigrant families throughout the Southland whose dreams of a better life are yet to be fulfilled. These families are part of an Asian population which has "increased by nearly five folds between 1970 and 1990, from roughly 190 thousand to approximately 926 thousand" (Ong and Azores, 1993, p. 1). They come from many walks of life, from many nations throughout Asia and the Pacific. Once here, they face a myriad of barriers and obstacles just to make a decent living, let alone achieve the dreams that led them here.

There is a large, often voiceless and invisible population of low-income Asians, mostly recent immigrants, in Los Angeles. Most are low income despite having a job -- they are part of the growing ranks of the working poor, earning wages that cannot support a decent standard of living. A significant proportion, especially among Southeast Asian refugees, are poor because they cannot find employment. These are families that depend primarily and often exclusively on welfare and other forms of public assistance, income that is barely enough for food and shelter.

Why do they find themselves in the situation they do? Low-income Asians are forced to accept low-wage jobs because they lack the skills to succeed in the job market. English proficiency is the biggest and most obvious barrier. Without English skills, job options are very limited. But in addition, large numbers of Asian immigrants come with little or no formal schooling. Many come from low socioeconomic backgrounds in their native country, and lack marketable job skills here in the U.S.

Many Vietnamese, Cambodian and other Southeast Asian refugees carry the scars of emotional and psychological trauma of violence, incarceration, disruption of families and harrowing escapes they experienced in their native lands. Given these experiences, it is not surprising that so many have difficulties adjusting and finding stable employment.

The lack of skills and psychological scars are hurdles faced by Asian immigrants as they try to make it here in the U.S. But beyond the problems individuals face are larger, structural obstacles. The Southland economy has been going through tremendous change over the past decade resulting in an expansion of low-wage, dead-end jobs and a sharp reduction of higher wage manufacturing jobs. This has constricted the opportunity for upward mobility because there are fewer and fewer better paying jobs. For thousands of poor Asians, the ladder of opportunity has been sheared off.

A significant proportion of these low-wage jobs are generated by the "ethnic economy," or by businesses owned by people of the same ethnicity as the worker. For recent immigrants with little English proficiency, such jobs are often their only option. Many of these businesses are small and operate on a thin margin. Wages and benefits generally are lower than in non-ethnic businesses, and immigrant workers often face exploitative working conditions.

All this adds up to a large and growing population of poor Asians throughout Los Angeles. While some are able, over time, to escape low income status, too many remain trapped because the individual and structural obstacles they face are too difficult to overcome. They are joined daily by new immigrants who come to reunite with families and to pursue their dreams of a better life, only to face the same barriers.

This population will continue to live at the margins unless greater action is taken. Their condition calls out for change, and challenges Asian American communities, policy-makers and the broader public to channel resources to empower low-income Asians to build a better future.

This chapter describes the conditions faced by low-income Asians in Los Angeles County, setting the stage for a discussion of approaches to empowerment in subsequent chapters.

Poverty Levels

According to the 1990 Census, there are over 124,000 Asians who are living in poverty in Los Angeles County. This represents 13 percent -- or one of every seven persons -- of the Asian American population, almost twice the proportion of non-Hispanic Whites who are in poverty. Chart 1 shows us poverty levels by ethnicity. There are even larger proportions of African Americans and Latinos below the poverty threshold.

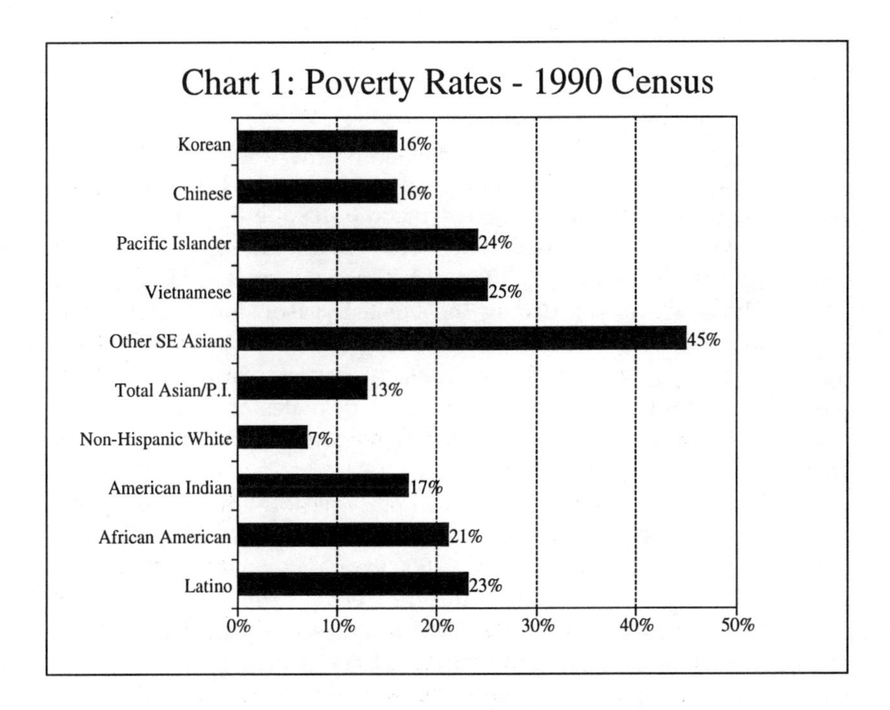

In 1989, the year for which income data was collected by the census, the poverty threshold for a family of four was $12,674. This comes out to an income of less than $1,056 per month. When one considers that the median rent in Los Angeles in 1990 was $626 (Shiver, 1992, p. D1), it becomes clear that a family can hardly afford to buy food, clothing and other basic necessities.

Poverty is not distributed evenly among different Asian ethnicities. As Chart 1 shows, the highest rates are for Southeast Asian refugees. Poverty for these populations is severe -- 10 percent of Vietnamese and

16 percent of Cambodian and Laotians live on incomes of $6,307 annually, less than 50 percent of the poverty threshold. Poverty among Pacific Islanders is also very high, with 12 percent living at less than 50 percent of the threshold.

The more recent the immigrant, the more likely they are to be in poverty. Of the Asians in poverty, two-thirds had immigrated since 1980. Moreover, families do not have to be under the poverty threshold to be poor. Low income levels just above the poverty threshold are also striking. Thirty-nine percent of ethnic Chinese from Southeast Asia make under $15,000 annual income, as do around one-quarter of Chinese, Korean, and Southeast Asians.

The Working Poor

Why are so many living at such low income levels? Most poor Asians cannot bring home a decent income despite the fact that they are employed. This includes many who are unable to find full-time, full year work. They can only find part-time jobs, or are only hired for part of the year, maybe during the busiest season for a retail store. Only about one-half of male and 27 percent of female Southeast Asian refugees work full-time, full year. Recent immigrants are more likely to be under-employed. About 55 percent of males and 32 percent of females who immigrated since 1985 have found full-time, full year work.

But many full-time Asian workers are low income as well. According to 1989-1991 Current Population Survey (CPS) data, 29 percent of Asian workers earned $15,000 annual income or less, despite the fact that they worked full-time, full year. This income is only slightly above poverty thresholds. In comparison, 27 percent of Non-Hispanic Whites, 39 percent of African Americans and 46 percent of Latinos had incomes of $15,000 or less.

Twenty-four percent of Asian workers (working at least half-time) make less than $7.50 per hour. At $7.50 per hour working 40 hours per week, a worker would only bring home $300 per week, or around $1,300 before taxes per month. Clearly, raising a family on this income is a tremendous hardship. There is a gender gap in wage levels as well, with 28 percent of female Asian workers making less than $7.50 compared to 21 percent of Asian males.

Recent Asian immigrants and refugees are more likely to be forced into such low-wage jobs than other Asians. Forty-four percent of ethnic Chinese from Southeast Asia, 32 percent of Koreans, 29 percent of

Southeast Asian refugees and 30 percent of Pacific Islanders make less than $7.50 per hour.

The Unemployed

While most low-income Asians are part of the working poor, there are also those who cannot find jobs. Overall, Asian Americans have relatively low unemployment rates. According to the 1990 Census, the Asian American unemployment rate in Los Angeles was 6.7 percent versus 7.4 percent for the County as a whole, 12 percent for African Americans and 10.1 percent for Latinos.

While Asians have high overall labor force participation rates, Census figures also show much lower rates for recent immigrants and refugees. Sixty-four percent of Asian males not in the labor force immigrated to the U.S. since 1980, as did 60 percent of Asian females. The ranks of the Asian jobless are dominated by Southeast Asian refugees in particular. Amost 30 percent of male and 57 percent of female refugees were not employed.

Because of the inability to find employment, large numbers of Southeast Asian refugees rely on public assistance for survival. There were close to 18,000 Asian and Pacific Islanders on welfare in Los Angeles County in 1992, and the majority were Southeast Asian refugees. Of the Asians on Aid to Families with Dependent Children (AFDC), 41 percent were Vietnamese and 30 percent were Cambodian (DPSS, 1992).

The inability to find work and consequently, the continued reliance on welfare is not just a temporary problem for refugees. According to a national study by Ngoan Le, 45 percent of Vietnamese, 44 percent of Lao and Hmong, and close to 100 percent of Cambodians are welfare-dependent after the first year of their resettlement (Le, 1993, p. 171). According to the federal Department of Health and Human Services, 79 percent of refugees in California are still dependent on welfare two years after arrival.

Among other racial minorities such as African Americans, there are high numbers of single-parent families, mostly single mothers, who cannot make enough money to support their children and consequently are forced onto the welfare rolls. Single-parent households are generally a rare occurrence among Asian Americans, except for Southeast Asian refugees. However, the majority of Southeast Asian refugee families on public assistance are two-parent families. Aid to Families with Dependent Children (AFDC) has two separate programs, one directed toward single-parent households, and another, AFDC-U, directed toward two-parent households. Asians represent the largest single ethnicity among AFDC-U recipients, at 34 percent, and they are virtually all Southeast Asian. It is not surprising that many minority single-parents are unable to bring home enough income to support their families without public assistance. But when large numbers of two-parent families are found on welfare rolls, this indicates extraordinarily severe obstacles to finding employment for these groups.

Low Job Skills

Why do so many Asian immigrants make such low wages? They come to the U.S. lacking the marketable skills necessary to get better, higher paying jobs. In particular, limited English capability limits their options for employment. Approximately one-half of those who speak English "not well" or "not at all" make under $15,000 yearly income. Sixty-nine percent of those who do not speak English at all earned less than $15,000. Without English skills, immigrants are locked out of a range of jobs that require dealing with the public, or with English-speaking co-workers. A lack of English proficiency can be an overwhelming barrier to basic survival. As a Vietnamese survey respondent in Long Beach explained, "I cannot go out far because I am afraid; I can't communicate, I don't know how to ask for directions or take the bus. . . anywhere I go I have to walk" (Luu interview, 1993).

While low English proficiency is probably the single largest barrier facing recent immigrants, their job options are also constrained by the level of schooling and job skills they bring from their native country. A significant number of Asian immigrants come from professional or managerial classes in Asia. But there are also equally large numbers who immigrate with low levels of schooling and job skills.

Typically, Pacific Islanders such as Samoans or Tongans come from low income backgrounds, with few job skills. Among Chinese, country of origin is an important factor in considering levels of education and job skills. While 65 percent of immigrants from Taiwan between 1983-86 had four or more years of university study, only 18 percent of immigrants had university schooling from mainland China, 25 percent from Hong Kong, and 27 percent from other countries such as Singapore, Vietnam, Macau, Burma and Malaysia (Hum and Ong, 1992, p. 25). Many immigrants with low levels of schooling in their home country come from low socioeconomic backgrounds and lack marketable job skills. According to the census, 51 percent of Asian Americans with less than a high school education make under $15,000, compared with only 12 percent of those with a B.A. or higher degree.

SALIC, our Survey of Asians in Low Income Communities, further illustrate the difficulties faced by immigrants who come from low-skill employment backgrounds in their native countries. Survey respondents who were self-employed, often individual street vendors in their native countries, have a current median annual income of only $7,920 here in the U.S. A sampling of survey respondents with a variety of low-skill and semi-skilled occupations in their native country (including service occupations, sales, clerical, laborers and garment work) revealed a median annual income of $8,196 in the U.S. This compares to survey respondents with a professional, technical or managerial background in their native country who currently have a median income of $15,000 in the U.S.

Significant numbers of Pacific Islanders, Southeast Asian and other recent immigrants come from countries that are predominantly rural. For these immigrants, adjusting to a fast-paced, modern urban environment is an even larger hurdle that will affect employment, housing and other survival needs (Tuione interview, 1992). Among survey respondents who were farmers in their native country, current median income was only $8,880. Close to 80 percent of those who were farmers in their native country were not working, reflecting severe difficulties finding employment.

Without marketable skills, these workers are locked into the low wage sector of the economy. According to CPS data, 49 percent of Asian workers are in typically low-wage sales, clerical and service occupations, with 13 percent in blue collar jobs (Hum and Ong, 1992, p. 40). Of the Asian men in the service category, 56 percent were in food preparation, which includes cooks, waiters and busboys. Of the women, 25 percent were in health services. In general, the gender gap also affects new immigrants. Asian women generally make only 80 cents for every dollar in wages of Asian men (Hum and Ong, 1992, p. 46).

In our survey areas, 45 percent of male respondents were in nonskilled, service, garment or sales occupations. Females were concentrated in fewer, but definitely low-wage occupations -- 52 percent were either in garment, sales or clerical/administrative support occupations.

In addition to low wages, high numbers of Asians in these jobs are also without medical coverage from their employers. Among all our survey respondents, 57 percent did not have medical coverage from their employers. These families are among the millions in the U.S. without health coverage -- for whom basic medical needs often go unmet, and for whom a major medical emergency can often bring economic ruin.

Southeast Asian Refugees

Southeast Asian refugees face the same obstacles as other recent immigrants but to an even greater degree. For example, learning English is very difficult due to high rates of illiteracy in their native languages. One-third of Cambodian and Laotian refugees are illiterate in their native languages (Le, 1993, pp. 172-3). Learning a new language is difficult enough, but it is even harder when one cannot read or write in their native language.

Employment skills vary with ethnicity and time of settlement. Earlier waves of Vietnamese refugees often came from high political, military or business positions in South Vietnam, but this is not the case for more recent waves of Vietnamese. Close to 40 percent of all Southeast Asian refugees were in farming or fishing in their native countries. In a study conducted in San Diego, 31 percent of Hmong interviewed had been in the military in their native country (Le, 1993, p. 179).

Refugees have also suffered through incredibly traumatic experiences just to make it to the U.S. A Vietnamese survey respondent living in Long Beach described how her family attempted an escape from Vietnam by boat just after she finished high school. They were caught and imprisoned for six months. Upon her release, she was forbidden to pursue higher education because of her "crime," and worked at a soap factory and as a cigarette vendor to support herself, her parents and a mentally handicapped younger sister. She and her family were finally brought to the U.S. in 1992 through the Orderly Departure Program under the sponsorship of her sister in Oklahoma. Fearful of her new and foreign environment, she never ventured outside the house during the two months she stayed there. She moved in May to Long Beach, but in doing so, lost her eligibility for government refugee support. Her family of four now lives solely on her younger handicapped sister's SSI disability grant. She cannot afford local ESL classes and has not been able to find a job.

Among Southeast Asian refugees are people who survived the "Killing Fields" in Cambodia, government persecution in Vietnam, and refugee camps in Thailand. A study of mental health among refugees in 1985 reported that 66 percent of Cambodians had lost at least one family member, 42 percent of Vietnamese had a family member jailed, and another 30 percent had been assaulted during their escape (Le, 1993, p. 180). These horrifying experiences have left many refugees suffering from depression, "post traumatic stress syndrome," and other serious mental health problems. Service providers at the Indochinese Refugee Counseling Center report that such emotional difficulties are often the primary obstacle to employment -- traumatized and fearful of their new environment, many are too afraid to even leave their homes (Indochinese Refugee interview, 1992). It is no surprise, therefore, that so many Southeast Asian refugees are without work and dependent on public assistance.

The Impact of Economic Restructuring

Limited English proficiency, the lack of job skills and the impact of severe emotional trauma are key factors limiting options of immigrants for decent employment. But at another level, there are structural factors that affect the employment options of Asian immigrants. In Southern California, the large and growing low-wage service, retail and light manufacturing sectors increasingly rely on immigrant labor, while the opportunities for better jobs are shrinking.

The Southland economy has been undergoing tremendous changes over the past two decades. Scholars have described the process as "economic restructuring." Through the 1960s and 1970s, U.S. capitalism accelerated the process of centralization and globalization. As multinational corporations became increasingly powerful, they have extended their scope of operations. Traditional U.S.-based forms of industrial manufacturing such as the high-wage, large-scale assembly line auto and steel plants, along with historic arrangements with the trade unions, became increasingly unattractive to these corporations.

Los Angeles was once the city with the second largest automobile assembly industry in the country. But in 1992, the last auto plant in the region, in Van Nuys, closed forever. In South Gate alone, the closures since 1980 of Firestone Rubber, General Motors and Norris Industries-Weiser Lock plants resulted in the loss of over 12,500 jobs (Soja, 1987, p. 182). According to the Bureau of Labor Statistics, U.S. Department of Labor, the Los Angeles region (Los Angeles-Long Beach SMSA) lost over 198,000 jobs in the durable manufacturing category from 1980 to 1992, a decline of 32 percent in this sector.

The industries with the greatest job losses were relatively high wage and highly unionized industries. To escape paying these wages, firms moved production facilities overseas or to other regions where wages and levels of unionization are lower. For instance, plants closed in Los Angeles by Uniroyal moved to Brazil and Turkey; Max Factor went to Tennessee; Litton Industries, Motorola, General Motors, Chrysler and Transitron moved to Mexico (Maxted and Zegeye, 1991, p. 234).

The aerospace and defense industries, along with other high-technology firms represented a huge growth industry during the 1970s and early 1980s. But with the end of the Cold War, major defense-related plant closings over the past couple of years marked the end of even more high wage, unionized production jobs as well as some professional and engineering positions.

In their place, the fastest growing industry in Los Angeles during the 1980s was the service sector, which grew by 36 percent from 1980 to 1992, an increase of 302,700 jobs. The service industry is now the largest sector in the Los Angeles economy. The service sector includes such jobs as hotel personnel, school teacher assistants, as well as various occupations in the largest part of the sector, business services and the health industry. Retail trades was also a major growth industry, adding over 38,000 jobs from 1980 to 1992 (this figure would be much higher were it not for temporary job losses due to the current recession).

"Nondurable" manufacturing saw modest growth during the 1980s. These include industries such as paper and printing, which, as mentioned before, help to service the corporate and financial headquarters. But the largest industry in this category is apparel, which saw a 30 percent job growth from 1980 to 1992. The garment industry is largely non-union and pays some of the lowest wages of any industry.

The overall economic restructuring has generated, on the one hand, an increase in elite, highly-paid managerial, banking, and administrative jobs, and, on the other hand, a much larger increase in low-paying service and retail jobs. These low-paying jobs include hotel and restaurant work, sales and clerical work, building maintenance personnel, as well as personal service workers such as maids, childcare workers, gardeners, etc. Meanwhile, higher-paying, unionized manufacturing jobs have all but disappeared. Selected 1992 median wage levels for occupations in declining and rising industries tell this story of wage disparities (Table 1).

TABLE 1: Wage Rates

Occupation	Median Wage: New hire; no experience	Median Wage: After 3 years with firm
Durable Manufacturing		
Machinists	$ 6.65	$15.00
Machine-tool operators	10.00	16.00
Welders & Cutters	8.50	12.00
Service, Retail, Nondurable Manufacturing		
Food preparation	$ 5.08	$ 6.84
Maids & Housekeeping	5.50	6.38
Sewing machine operators	4.25	7.00

Source: Employment Development Department, Los Angeles County, June 1992

The massive flows of legal and illegal immigrants from Mexico, Central and Latin America, and Asia have filled many of the new low-wage service and light manufacturing jobs. To become competitive in the global market, these industries rely on immigrant workers who have no choice but to accept "Third World" level wages and working conditions. Better paying jobs require higher levels of education and technical skills that put them out of reach of most immigrant workers. Thus, the structure of the Southland economy channels many Asian immigrants into the low-wage job market.

Persistent Poverty?

In identifying an appropriate response to the problems we have described, the key question is whether the economic hardship that Asian immigrants face is a temporary or ongoing phenomenon. If the problem is temporary, then traditional social services will help immigrants through rough times. But from all indications, this problem is not a temporary phenomenon. There are two main reasons for this conclusion: 1) the flow of low-skill immigrants from Asia will continue into the future, and 2) a large proportion of today's low-income families will be locked into their economic situation.

There is no reason to assume that the flow of immigration from Asia and the Pacific to the U.S. will slow in the future. Based on current population trends, Paul Ong and Suzanne Hee estimate an increase in the foreign-born Asian population of anywhere from 110 to 141 percent by the year 2020 (Ong and Hee, 1993, pp. 18-19). Further, between 80 to 90 percent of Asian immigration to the U.S. is through family reunification (Hing, 1993, p. 129). As stated earlier, Asians who are low income in the U.S. often come from low socioeconomic backgrounds in their native country. Now that they are here, many will want to bring their siblings and relatives. It is reasonable to assume that a large proportion of these relatives will also be from low socioeconomic backgrounds. These new immigrants will therefore face the same job disadvantages as their predecessors.

While the total numbers allowed into the U.S. under refugee categories have been decreasing, refugees, once here, usually want to bring their relatives over. Many of these relatives are likely to be from low socioeconomic backgrounds and have suffered through traumatic experiences in their native country.

The conventional wisdom is that we should not worry about the continuous influx of low-skill immigrants into the country. According to this view, the history of America demonstrates that low-income immigrants will, after a few years here, learn English, find better jobs and move out of low-income communities. While it is debatable whether this view was ever the historical pattern for immigrants, there are clear indications that today it is not applicable. Undoubtedly, many immigrants will, through hard work and a little luck, achieve significant upward mobility. But we believe large numbers will be locked into their difficult economic situation. The key factors are 1) their limited English proficiency, 2) their lack of opportunities for advancement, and 3) their existence in an economy with a shrinking number of better-paying jobs.

Low English proficiency will continue to be a major barrier to upward mobility for many immigrants. Limited availability and access to ESL instruction makes it difficult for recent immigrants to improve their language skills. For those working in the ethnic economy, there is often little incentive to learn English since their native language is the primary language on the job. But as long as English proficiency is low, the chance for upward mobility will be slim.

Second, the low-wage, low-skill jobs held by poor Asians offer little opportunity for advancement. As a housekeeper in a hotel, a garment seamstress, or a food server in a restaurant, there is not much opportunity to learn new skills that can enable a worker to find higher paying jobs.

If conventional wisdom were correct, recent immigrants in low-wage occupations should have been able to get better jobs after several years. Table 2 shows the occupational distribution of SALIC respondents who have lived in the U.S. ten years and under, and over ten years. For both groups, there are about the same percentages of workers in low-wage unskilled and service occupations, and in clerical/administrative support which includes both low and medium wage jobs. While these are not longitudinal results (i.e., following the same individuals over time), they indicate that even after ten years in the U.S., many are still stuck in low wage occupations.

Of those workers who have been in the U.S. longer than ten years (excluding professionals, technicians and managers), one-half still make less than $8.00 per hour. Although this is an improvement over the median wage of $5.50 for workers in the same occupations here ten years or less, it shows that there are large numbers of long-term workers who are still bringing home low wages.

TABLE 2: Occupational Distribution

	Percent Lived in U.S.	
Occupation	10 years or less	over 10 years
Prof/Tech/Mgr	22%	33%
Cler/Admin support	21%	20%
Sales	10%	4%
Service*	15%	17%
Skilled labor**	8%	11%
Unskilled labor***	19%	16%
Other	0%	3%

*Service includes restaurant, domestic, personal/cleaning and other services
**Skilled labor includes craft occupations and electrical assistants
***Unskilled labor includes operators, laborers, gardeners, driver/deliverers, garment

Source: Survey of Asians in Low-Income Communities, 1993.

Another measure of upward mobility is the extent of wage improvement between a respondent's current job and his/her previous job. If conventional wisdom were correct, those who have been here ten years or more should have been able to significantly improve their wages from one job to the next. But in our survey, 48 percent saw their wages improve only $1.00 or less from their previous job. For those here ten years or less, 63 percent experienced wage improvement of less than $1.00. Thus, even among those who have been in the U.S. for some time, many are unable to significantly improve their pay from one job to the next.

A final reason why many low-income Asians will still be locked in low-wage jobs even after a substantial amount of time in the U.S. relates to the state of the Los Angeles economy. The number of high-paying jobs will likely continue to shrink. Significant proportions of previous waves of Asian immigrants may well have experienced substantial upward mobility over time. Immigrants entering the U.S. following the 1965 immigration reform through the mid-1970s entered a growing economy, still pre-eminent in the world in many respects. Immigrants coming in during the 1980s and 1990s, however, face a very different situation.

As discussed earlier in the chapter, economic restructuring has resulted in a small increase in very high-paying jobs, accessible only to those with a substantial amount of education, and a much larger increase in low-wage jobs in the service, retail and light manufacturing sectors. Meanwhile, there has been a decrease in the number of medium wage jobs. There are simply fewer and fewer well-paying jobs that low-wage workers can advance into, without a graduate or professional degree.

According to the Employment Development Department (EDD), these economic trends will continue into the future. Based on their projections, by 1997, the service industry will grow by 12 percent and the retail trades will gain 51,200 workers, while durable manufacturing will continue to decline with over 81,000 job losses (EDD, 1992, p. 15).

Conclusion: New Policies and Action

If the phenomenon of Asians living on desperately low incomes only involved a small number of people, or was only a temporary "adjustment" period for immigrants, then short-term strategies would be adequate. But it is clear that the problem in Los Angeles County is neither small nor temporary. The depth and scope of this population demands attention and action. The remainder of this book addresses these concerns.

CHAPTER THREE

Inner-City Communities

Everything is convenient. There is no need for transportation. You walk and you find stores you need. My parents like living here because they can't speak English. Here everyone speaks Chinese. Food is good. It is close to my company so I don't have to drive too far. I like it here.

Chinatown resident

The quotation reveals some of the reasons why many Asians choose to live in ethnic enclaves. Whether for cultural and linguistic need, social networks, job opportunities, or lack of other options, many low-income Asians are geographically concentrated in growing Asian communities throughout Los Angeles County. But unlike the self-defined, enclosed ethnic ghettos typified by San Francisco's Chinatown, Asian enclaves in Los Angeles share space with other races, have no clear geographic boundaries, and are dispersed throughout the county. This intermingling of races and loosely-defined geographic community raise unique complexities that must be addressed in any Asian Community Economic Development strategy.

The first major wave of Asian immigrants to this region during the latter half of the nineteenth century to the early part of this century established many Asian communities in Los Angeles. They formed enclaves such as Chinatown and Little Tokyo and their more rural counterparts, such the Japanese community in Gardena, as survival mechanisms against racism. These neighborhoods served as economic and cultural bases for these populations. After World War II, Asians were able to move out of these enclaves, as racially-based legal and social restrictions on housing eased. This was particularly true for the better educated and higher skilled Asians who had the financial means to relocate to the predominantly white suburbs. The result was a separation of the rich and poor Asians, with low-income immigrants and the elderly remaining as the primary residents of inner-city enclaves. Moreover, these communities were slowly dying, because there were too few new immigrants to replace those leaving.

The renewal of large-scale immigration after the 1965 Immigration Act and the influx of refugees from Southeast Asian have revitalized inner-city Asian neighborhoods and have created new concentrations in the suburbs. As Table 1 shows, the rapid growth of the Asian population in the last three decades corresponds with the increasing concentration of Asian Americans. While "Asian neighborhoods" are becoming more visible, Asians are still the least segregated race in Los Angeles. Only one percent of Asians live in census tracts where they comprise at least 80 percent of the residents (Ong and Azores, 1993, p. 27). In comparison, about one-third of Anglos, one-fourth of Latinos, and one-fifth of African Americans reside in areas where they comprise such a dominant concentration (Ong and Azores, 1993, p. 27). The lack of hyper-segregation for Asians is due to both the ethnic and class heterogeneity, which tends to produce many smaller population centers rather than one or two large communities.

TABLE 1: Distribution of Asians by Neighborhood Type

Percent Asian	1970		1990		1970-90
in Neighborhood	No.	%	No.	%	% Incr.
0-9%	107,315	58.9	251,989	27.8	135
10-19%	39,189	21.0	243,296	26.8	521
20-29%	17,068	9.1	163,660	18.1	775
30-49%	18,702	10.0	196,327	21.7	950
over 50%	4,711	2.5	51,273	5.7	988

Source: Ong & Azores, 1993.

In addition to the more established communities, newer communities have developed within the last three decades throughout the metropolitan area. The sprawling communities of the West San Gabriel Valley (Rosemead, El Monte, Monterey Park, and Alhambra) are home to Chinese and Vietnamese. Carson is the home to one of the largest Filipino communities. Pomona has a large concentration of low-income Laotians and Cambodians. Near the Los Angeles Airport, in Lennox and Inglewood, is a thriving Tongan community. Lynwood and South Gate contain pockets of Laotians. Compton is home to a large community of Samoans. The Hollywood area has a significant Thai community, as well as many Filipinos and Laotians. Sections of the San Fernando Valley are home to low-income Vietnamese and other Asians.

Not all Asian enclaves are residential neighborhoods. Little Tokyo, which is south of downtown, is primarily a commercial and cultural center. With relatively small numbers of new Japanese immigrants coming to Los Angeles, this neighborhood has few residents, most of whom are low-income Japanese American senior citizens. On the other hand, it has a large number of restaurants, retail stores, cultural facilities, and service organizations, which serve tourists and the larger Japanese American population in Los Angeles.

Although Asian enclaves are no longer just low-income communities, there is still a spatial segregation by class. While many of the newer suburban enclaves are middle-class, the inner-city neighborhoods continue to be primarily low-income, predominantly immigrant communities. Despite tremendous needs that overwhelm community-based agencies, and city and county departments, low-income Asians continue to be attracted by the basic support networks often available only in inner-city enclaves.

Despite the increasing concentration of Asians in the inner-city, today's enclaves have the added complexity of intermingling with non-Asian neighbors. Latinos constitute the largest racial group in both inner-city Los Angeles and Long Beach.

The concentration of low-income Asians often creates as well as exacerbates individual and social problems. Large numbers of low-income persons increase the competition for limited community resources such as jobs, affordable housing, and social services. The stress and struggle for survival may weaken family and social relationships, fostering mental and physical health problems, crime, gang activity, substance abuse, as well as domestic violence and other family problems.

Yet at the same time, geographic concentration represents potential strength through the sheer numbers of Asian residents with common problems and aspirations. Since Asians still constitute a small proportion of the population in most places, they are generally without a political voice. Numerical strength offers opportunities to organize a community and to develop a common agenda in seeking changes to improve the basic living conditions of low-income Asians and other community members.

Chapter Two summarized the general problems and issues facing low-income Asians. This chapter continues to examine these problems by taking a more indepth look at three specific geographic communities and the living conditions of their Asians residents. These communities are greater Chinatown, Koreatown/Westlake, and Long Beach. These enclaves contain concentrations of the largest Asian ethnic groups in the county, demonstrate different stages of community growth, and permit comparisons between immigrant and refugee populations. Thus, while these communities are representative of Asian enclaves, their unique characteristics remind us that understanding specific as well as general community needs is crucial to defining the role of Community Economic Development.

Characteristics of Three Asian Inner-City Communities

Chinatown, Koreatown/Westlake, and south Long Beach are representative of the many low-income Asian communities in Los Angeles County. According to 1990 Census data, these three communities housed nearly one-quarter of all Asians living in poverty in the county. These enclaves are primarily immigrants communities, where over two-thirds of the Asians are foreign-born. The U.S.-born tend to be the children of immigrant parents. A large proportion of the adults are recent Asian immigrants and refugees with limited English-speaking abilities. Few have marketable job skills, especially the large numbers of Southeast Asian refugees with farming backgrounds and little formal education. Yet despite similarities, each community has its own characteristics and needs.

Chinatown is one of the more established Asian communities in Los Angeles, but it is no longer confined to its old boundaries north of downtown. Today, greater Chinatown, which is defined as the area served by its many social service agencies as well as by the ethnicity of the residents, includes parts of Echo Park to the west and Lincoln Heights to the east. The Asian population in this area is about 20,000. While Chinatown is still predominantly Chinese, the area has undergone major demographic changes with the influx of Vietnamese and Cambodian residents. Although the business core of Chinatown is well defined by Bernard, Alameda, Sunset, and Hill Streets, the residential area extends into parts of Lincoln Heights and Echo Park.

Koreatown/Westlake is the largest of the three inner-city communities both in geographic area and population. In addition to the more visible Koreans, significant numbers of Filipino residents and businesses, as well as other Asians, call this area home. Although established after Chinatown, Asian communities in this area are expanding rapidly.

Although Koreans have been in Los Angeles since the early half of this century, Koreatown is a creation of the post-1965 immigration. Koreans represent one of the fastest growing populations in Los Angeles County. In the 1970s, the Olympic/Normandie area represented Koreatown. By 1980, Koreatown boundaries had expanded to Wilshire, Hoover, Pico, and Crenshaw. Today, Koreatown continues to grow, most notably to the north. This enclave in the mid-city area west of downtown is home to over 30,000 Asians. Although Korean immigrants comprise the dominant group in this enclave, there are also significant numbers of Filipinos, Thais, and other Asian ethnicities. Besides serving local residents, Koreatown's businesses, restaurants, churches, and social associations attract Koreans and other Asians from all over the area.

The Filipino community in the greater downtown area of Los Angeles originated in the 1920s. Although urban renewal displaced residents from their initial location, the community has survived. This "new" Filipino concentration was created in the 1950s when the Bunker Hill redevelopment plan forced residents and businesses to move from the small "Manilatown" near downtown, bordered by San Pedro Street, Figueroa, and Sunset Boulevard. Today, Filipinotown, located roughly between Chinatown and Koreatown, includes parts of Westlake, Echo Park, and Silverlake, and exists as a residential pocket for over 15,000 Filipinos. While we call this area "Filipinotown," the concentration of residents and businesses is less apparent than in enclaves like Chinatown or Koreatown, which have a strong ethnic identity because of the vast number of Asian-owned businesses and community institutions. Filipinotown has only a few visible landmarks located in its core area around Temple Street and Beverly Boulevard. Its commercial sector is largely absent, and its community institutions are not highly visible.

This may be partly due to Filipino adoption of American culture and the English language due to years of U.S. colonialism, resulting in relatively less need of an ethnic enclave. However, with new immigration, concentrations of Filipinos are increasing, indicating both a desire for a cultural community as well as economic problems. For despite a generally higher average education and skill level compared to other Asians, Filipinos live barely above the poverty line due to underemployment and relatively limited skills. The concentration of

Filipinos is still highest in Filipinotown, but smaller settlements have formed in Cerritos, West Covina, and Carson.

Unlike the older ethnic enclaves, Cambodians did not establish a community in Long Beach until about 1975. A small group of Cambodians, who arrived in Long Beach as exchange students in the 1960s, paved the way for the settlement of refugees after the Khmer Rouge seized control of Cambodia. After refugees were processed at nearby Camp Pendleton, Long Beach became a natural destination. Many refugees who had heard of the area through exchange students wanted to settle in California and found the supply of housing abundant after the navy moved to San Diego. Today, Long Beach has the highest residental concentration of Cambodians outside Cambodia. The heaviest concentration is within a section of South Long Beach bounded by Magnolia and Redondo, and 7th Street and Willow. This is home to nearly 15,000 Cambodians, making it the largest Cambodian community in the country. Along with its residential base, the community has a very visible commercial sector.

Significant numbers of Asians living in these inner-city communities are immigrants, often accounting for 80 to 90 percent of the population.[1] Although a slightly greater proportion of Asians in inner-city Los Angeles are immigrants compared with those in Long Beach, Southeast Asian communities are those most likely to consist of mainly foreign-born.

Of the immigrants, most are "recent" arrivals with ten or fewer years of residency in the U.S. Because of the political chaos that forced many to seek asylum in the U.S., Southeast Asians have the highest proportion of newcomers in Los Angeles and Long Beach, with 70 percent arriving between 1980 and 1990. However, in Long Beach, Southeast Asians have an even higher proportion of newcomers, approximately 85 percent, showing that distinctions exist even among Southeast Asian populations. The difference may be explained by the fact that most Southeast Asians in Long Beach are Cambodians who settled in the U.S. primarily after 1979, while most in inner-city Los Angeles are Vietnamese who came in two major waves in 1975 and 1979.

After Southeast Asians, Koreans and Filipinos have the next highest proportion of recent arrivals at about 65 and 55 percent respectively. Koreans and Filipinos have the highest proportion of very recent immigrants (those arriving between 1985 and 1990) since the unusually dramatic influx of Southeast Asians occurred only between the mid-1970s and early 1980s.

The proportion of very recent Asian immigrants range from 20-30 percent in Long Beach to 20-45 percent in inner-city Los Angeles. In Long Beach, the proportion is similar for both Filipinos and Southeast Asians immigrants: 30 percent. While the rate is lower for Southeast Asians in Los Angeles (20 percent), nearly 45 percent of Koreans are very recent immigrants, followed by Filipinos and Chinese at about 40 and 30 percent respectively.

While the proportion in each age group is similar among Asian ethnicities in the inner-cities, Southeast Asians in general and Asians in Long Beach tend to have a larger youth population and fewer older adults. Over 80 percent of Southeast Asians in both Los Angeles inner-city and Long Beach are under 45, compared to less than 70 percent for other Asian ethnicities. The proportion of youth among Southeast Asians is even more significant in Long Beach, where nearly 30 percent are under ten, and almost 50 percent are under 18 years old.

Even excluding Southeast Asians, more than 25 percent of Asians in Long Beach are under 18, compared with 20 percent in inner-city Los Angeles. By the same token, Southeast Asians and Asians in Long Beach, in general, have a smaller proportion of older adults.

Poverty Rates for Asians in the Inner-City

Low-income Asians tend to concentrate in the inner-cities. The poverty rate in the inner-city is higher than that for Asians in the county overall. Over 20 percent of Asians in both the Los Angeles inner-city and the City of Long Beach live below the poverty level, compared to 13 percent for Asians in the county. In addition, another 10 percent live barely above poverty with incomes of 1.5 times the poverty line. Poverty heavily burdens the young in the inner-cities, with one in three Asian children under 18 living in poverty.

Southeast Asians have the highest poverty rate in both the City of Los Angeles and Long Beach. Over 40 percent of Southeast Asians live in poverty. Another one-fourth have barely enough income to stay above the poverty line (up to 1.5 times the poverty level). The pattern of immigration among Southeast Asians explains much of their current employment and adjustment problems. Only 22 percent came to the U.S. between 1975 and 1979. Most of this first wave were refugees with high educational and employment backgrounds. However, over one-half arrived between 1980 and 1984, representing a second wave of mostly low-skilled farmers with very little education.

Despite media images on the economic success of Korean and Chinese Americans, one out of four Koreans and Chinese in the inner-city lives in poverty. Only Filipinos have poverty rates equal to the 7 percent for Non-Hispanic whites. The low poverty rate is partly explained by the larger number of workers in Filipino households, compared to other Asians.

Although individuals and families can barely live on poverty level income, many Asians do not even earn half of that income. Fifteen percent of Southeast Asians struggle to survive on less than half of poverty level income. The concentration of low-income Asians in certain geographic locations severely strains community resources, and desperately underscores the need for an economic development strategy.

Lack of Job Skills

The high incidence of poverty and low-income status among Asian immigrants, especially recent ones, is partly attributed to lack of English proficiency and low educational attainment. Recent arrivals have less earning potential than native-born Americans or immigrants who have settled in the U.S. for a long period of time. While almost one-third of Asians born in the U.S. earn less than $15,000 annually, the rate is two-thirds for immigrants with less than five years of residency. The higher proportion of recent Asian immigrants (those with ten years or less in the U.S.) who are not in the labor force (NILF) is similar in the inner-city.

Responses from our survey (SALIC, 1993) for Chinatown demonstrate the relationship between English speaking ability and earning power. Respondents rating themselves as speaking no English have an annual median income of $5,400. While those who speak "not well" do not fare any better, respondents who speak English "well" and "very well" have median incomes of $12,000 and $20,000 respectively. In a community where two out of three respondents believe they cannot speak English well, income is correspondingly low. Only 11 percent of SALIC respondents in Chinatown speak English very well.

Compared to Chinatown and Long Beach, fewer residents in Koreatown and Filipinotown have limited English speaking skills. The 40 percent with limited English capability is balanced somewhat by the 60 percent who speak well or very well. Since only 33 percent of Koreatown and Filipinotown respondents have taken ESL classes, the lower incidence of English training may be due to less need or lack of classes.

With little communication skills, Southeast Asians believe themselves "less accepted," increasing their difficulty in adjusting to a multicultural society. More than 55 percent of SALIC respondents rate themselves as speaking English not well or worse, although a similar percentage to residents in Koreatown had taken ESL classes. Only 14 percent believe they speak English very well.

Like residents of Koreatown and Filipinotown, Long Beach Asian residents show a similar relationship between English speaking ability and earning power. SALIC (1993) results reveal little change in median income among Asian residents in Koreatown, Filipinotown, and south Long Beach with different levels of English speaking capability. Yet the range of incomes is broader for better English speaking residents. In these communities, Asian respondents who do not speak English well have annual incomes up to $24,000. Those who speak English very well have incomes up to $38,400.

Low educational attainment exacerbates the lack of English skills. Among the Asian ethnicities, Southeast Asians and Chinese have the lowest educational attainment in both inner-city Los Angeles and Long Beach. Almost half of Southeast Asians and Chinese have not graduated from high school, compared with the 22 percent of inner-city Asians in general. Southeast Asians in Long Beach have more education than their counterparts in inner-city Los Angeles. Filipinos generally have higher educational attainment. Educational attainment is lowest for recent and very recent immigrants.

Many inner-city Asians with little formal education are not in the labor market (NILF). About one-half of Asians with less than a high school education are not in the labor force. Due to their limited English speaking ability and low skills, there is a high proportion of jobless inner-city Asians. Cambodians in Long Beach have the lowest level of economic activity, with a majority not in the labor force. Koreans and Chinese in inner-city Los Angeles have similar NILF rates, about 30 percent, but the Filipino rate is noticeably lower, about 10 percent.

Labor force participation also differs by gender and age. The Asian female NILF rate is double that of men in Long Beach and triple that of men in inner-city Los Angeles. On the other hand, with so many women not even in the labor force, the female unemployment rate is generally lower than that of males in both areas. While the youth NILF rate is similar to other age groups, youth between 18 and 24 have a high unemployment rate, nearly double that of others. The low labor force participation of Asian women and high unemployment of Asian youth demonstrate that programs to increase employability must specifically target these two groups.

Because of low skills, having a job for these immigrants does not guarantee a living wage. About half of Chinese and Koreans in the Los Angeles inner-city communities and Cambodians in Long Beach earn less than $15,000 annually. About 25 percent of Chinese and Koreans in inner-city Los Angeles and over 35 percent of Cambodians in Long Beach earn between $15,000 and $30,000 annually.

Although Filipinos may not be the poorest Asians, a higher percentage have low earnings compared to other Asians. About one-third of Filipinos earn less than $15,000, compared to the overall Asian rate of 44 percent. But over four-fifths of Filipinos in inner-city Los Angeles earn less than $30,000. Thus, despite better English speaking ability, higher educational attainment, and better labor force participation, Filipinos earn a modest living, compared to other Asians. In fact, the proportion of Filipinos earning less than $30,000 annually is larger than all other Asian ethnicities, except Southeast Asians.

About 20 percent of the Southeast Asian and Chinese populations work in the low-wage service sector. Southeast Asian in Los Angeles and Cambodians in Long Beach also display differences in occupational orientation. About 13 percent of Los Angeles' inner-city Southeast Asians are in managerial occupations and about 5 percent are in professional and technical fields. Yet, the inverse is true for Long Beach Cambodians.

Koreans have a different occupational orientation from other inner-city Asians. A higher proportion work in the managerial field than other Asians. However, while 16 percent have managerial careers, only 8 percent work in the professional or technical fields. Unlike other Asians, less than 9 percent are clerks, but 27 percent (more than double the Asian rate) work in sales-related jobs.

The entrepreneurship orientation of Koreans and generally better English speaking abilities of Koreans and Filipinos seem to reduce the correlation between English speaking ability and income in Koreatown and Filipinotown. Unlike Chinatown, where better English speaking abilities are correlated with higher incomes, no significant improvement exists in the incomes of Koreatown and Filipinotown Asians. However, income ranges vary greatly for those with better English skills. Asian residents who do not speak English had similar incomes, between $15,600 and $16,800. The potential to earn more seems higher for those who speak English well, with an income range from $3,600 to $30,000.

Those who speak very well had the greatest range, from $7,200 to $96,000.

Unlike other Asians in the inner-city or Long Beach, Filipinos in both areas suffer few of the more obvious economic survival problems. The poverty rate of Filipinos is similar to that of Non-Hispanic whites. Nearly 90 percent of Filipinos are in the labor force. Most Filipinos hold higher education degrees, and less than 10 percent do not have a high school diploma. Among the half who have at least a college degree, nearly 10 percent have master's or professional degrees.

Filipinos have an undistinguished occupational and earnings profile despite their English capabilities and educational attainment. The proportion of Filipinos in the managerial field is similar to other Asians. And while a good number have professional or technical jobs (over 15 percent), one out of three Filipinos holds clerical positions.

The Enclave Economy and Low-Wage Jobs

One of the attractions of living in an ethnic enclave is the availability of jobs which match the limited skills and resources of Asian immigrants. But the status also has negative consequences when employers exploit menial labor through low compensation, poor working conditions, and little opportunity for upward mobility.

Each of our three communities has characteristics of both an ethnic and enclave economies. Ethnic economies thrive by exploiting low-skill immigrant labor for the production of goods and services for the general population. Asian-owned factories in garment, restaurant and other industries can easily fill their labor needs with the vast numbers of limited English speaking immigrants who have no other job choices. On the other hand, Asian enclave economies that target customers in ethnic communities, pay low wages because most are small businesses with narrow profit margins.

Because of the capital needed to start businesses, more Asian employers are found in inner-city Los Angeles than in the newer and poorer Cambodian community in south Long Beach. The 14 percent rate of self-employment or working in a family business for Asians in Los Angeles' inner-city is almost double that of Asians in Long Beach. Entrepreneurship is low among very recent Asian immigrants (those living in U.S. five years or less) and those with low educational attainment, regardless of their area or ethnicity. This may be due to lack of financial and other resources, limited language and business skills, as well as unfamiliarity with U.S. business practices.

All the Asian communities studied have businesses which cater to particular ethnic groups. Chinatown and Koreatown have the most visible number of businesses. Possibly due to their generally better English fluency, Filipinos in both Long Angeles and Long Beach lack an ethnic commercial center despite their long tenure in these areas. Less than 5 percent of Filipinos are self-employed or work in a family business. Although a much newer community, Cambodians in Long Beach have established a number of businesses whose market is the ethnic enclave.

Due to their more limited resources as poor refugees, Cambodians tend to operate small businesses with low overhead and skill requirements such as donut shops, restaurants, grocery stores, garages, and gift shops. Many of these small business owners function as they had in Cambodia with no credit, few loans, and no accounting system (Pok, 1992). As is true with other ethnic enclave businesses, Cambodian small businesses face high competition and concentration in a few food, retail and service businesses.

Koreans in Los Angeles' inner-city account for much of the high Asian rate of entrepreneurship, as over a quarter are either self-employed or in family businesses. But a majority of Korean businesses are small family-owned and operated firms. Thus, they too offer mostly low-wage jobs, if any jobs at all.

The large numbers of small businesses in ethnic enclave economies means that job opportunities are meager and wages are likely to be low. Small businesses generally have very small profit margins. And because of the lack of diversity among the types of businesses, competition further reduces profit resulting in jobs with very low wages and no job security.

Lack of Affordable Housing

Asians, like other low-income populations throughout the county, face a massive affordable housing crisis. For thousands of low-income Asian families, high rents and mortgages are an additional burden in the quest for financial security.

The major reason for high rents and mortgages is the inadequate supply of affordable housing. For example, the City of Los Angeles grows an average of over 26,000 households every year, but developers generate only 15,000 housing units (Housing Preservation and Production Department (HPPD), 1991, pp. 11-13). After considering the average annual demolition of 3,000 units, we are left with a 14,000 unit shortfall every year. And the shortfall is greatest for affordable housing units. As a result, HPPD data indicates that more than 150,000 families in the City of Los Angeles spend more than half their income on rent.

The current rent and mortgage levels severely strain family budgets of the unemployed, working poor, and in particular, welfare recipients. Federal guidelines from the Department of Housing and Urban Development identify 30 percent of household income as the ceiling for an "affordable" amount to pay for housing. Paying more than 30 percent reduces expenditure for food, clothing, and other necessities. Median rent in Los Angeles was $626 in 1990 (Shiver, 1992). In order to afford this rent at 30 percent of their income, household members need to earn a total of $2,087 per month. In Los Angeles County, 32 percent of Asian households earn less than that amount, according to the 1990 Census. The brunt of the affordable housing burden falls on low-income communities. Approximately two-thirds of renters surveyed in our three communities paid more than the "affordable" rent. Much of this high rate is attributable to the low incomes and high rents of Southeast Asians in south Long Beach and greater Chinatown.

The spiraling cost of homeownership puts this out of reach for most low-income families and even many middle-income families. Between 1980 and 1990, home prices in Los Angeles County shot up 157 percent, resulting in a median home price of $226,400 (Shiver, 1992). Median mortgage payments increased correspondingly to $1,137 per month, an amount greater than the total income of many low-income families. Because of the low income of most Southeast Asians, the relatively lower home prices of $150,000 in south Long Beach do not help the refugee population attain homeownership.

Avoiding high housing costs often means living in overcrowded or substandard residences. An estimated 200,000 families double or triple up with other families in cramped apartments throughout the City of Los Angeles (HPPD, 1991, p. 13). The Los Angeles Housing Preservation and Production Department's overcrowded standard is more than two persons per room (excluding kitchen and bathroom). Almost one in five of the SALIC households lived in overcrowded units. Asians in south Long Beach have the severest problem with about 30 percent living in such units. Many Southeast Asian households in inner-city Los Angeles have six or more members. Hardly any Southeast Asians live alone, compared to about 20 percent for other Asian ethnicities. Unfortunately, the genocide in Cambodia reduces the chances that Cambodians can share housing with extended families rather than non-family members. The greater Chinatown area and Koreatown have the next highest rates of overcrowding, about 50 percent and 20 percent respectively. Probably due to their slightly better income levels and higher labor force participation rates, few Asians in Koreatown and Filipinotown live in overcrowded conditions or pay a substantial amount of their incomes for rent.

In conducting our survey (SALIC, 1993), we found low-income Asian families living in horrid conditions: small, deteriorating backlot units, possibly illegally converted garages, and apartment buildings with trash lining dimly lit hallways. While residences in Koreatown tend to be newer, the attractive exterior facades often hide desolate courtyards and corridors. Koreatown and Filipinotown contain more large apartment complexes than greater Chinatown and south Long Beach, where housing consists primarily of detached houses and small apartment buildings. SALIC respondents in south Long Beach probably live in the worst conditions of those we studied. Although many live in apartment complexes with an almost communal environment, the buildings are run-down and flimsy. Children play in barren, dirt courtyards.

Conclusion: The Need to Improve the Quality of Life for Low-Income Asians

Without Community Economic Development, the concentration of low-income Asians in ethnic enclaves simply means competition for low-wage jobs and a small number of affordable housing units. The struggle to survive is intense, as the immigrants, especially recent arrivals, increase the labor pool of workers with limited English capabilities and few marketable skills. Their only employment option is in ethnic enclave businesses that provide low-wage, dead-end jobs. With a large number of immigrants in low-wage jobs and a sizeable proportion without jobs, employers are under little pressure to offer better wages, benefits, or job security. Compounding the low wages and joblessness is the lack of quality affordable housing. After paying more than they can afford for housing, low-income Asians have little left for other necessities.

NOTES

1. Unless otherwise noted, these statistics and those in the rest of the chapter are taken from tabulations of the 1990 Public Use Microdata Sample. Because the data provide only limited sub-county geographic identification, we gathered information for Koreans, Chinese, Filipinos, and Southeast Asians in the inner-city area of Los Angeles City, and for Cambodians for Long Beach. Although the data on Cambodians is for the entire City of Long Beach, they provide a picture of the Cambodians in the enclave, where a vast majority reside.

CHAPTER FOUR

Entrepreneurship and Enclave Economy

Looking at the broad picture, one wonders if the vision associated with owning one's own business is as much an illusion as the "American Dream" in the Asian psyche.

Khai T. Tran, student author of case study on a Vietnamese-owned business

By several measures, Asian entrepreneurship in Los Angeles is extensive. In the late 1980s, Asian-owned enterprises comprised 44 percent of all minority-owned businesses in this metropolitan area. Moreover, one out of every five Asian-owned firms in the United States can be found in the Los Angeles County. The emergence of this Asian entrepreneurial class suggests that with personal sacrifice and ingenuity, American ideals of self-reliance and personal independence are attainable. The uneven nature of Asian small business development, however, indicates that business ownership does not guarantee the kind of economic freedom and success that many Asian immigrants have come to expect. Asian businesses are typically family-based enterprises that rely on the unpaid labor of family members. These small establishments tend to be concentrated in highly competitive and marginal economic sectors where the threat of bankruptcy and/or substitution of product or services is high. These business conditions means that profit margins are slim, the work environment is poor, and overall benefits for workers and society-at-large are scarce.

Characteristics of Asian Businesses in Los Angeles

The period after the 1965 Immigration Act resulted in the mass influx of new immigrants, which transformed and revitalized Asian communities in the United States. This new growth was evident in the dramatic expansion of Asian businesses in Los Angeles County. (See Table 1.) For every firm that had operated in 1977, four firms operated in 1987. For some ethnic groups, namely the Koreans and Vietnamese, the expansion was particularly pronounced. Over the-ten year period, the number of Korean-owned enterprises grew by nearly seven-fold (676 percent). In 1977, there were not enough Vietnamese-owned store to warrant a separate listing, but in the five-year period between 1982 and 1987, their ranks grew by an astonishing 647 percent.

TABLE 1: Asian-Owned Businesses in LA County

	1977		1987		% Growth 1977-87
Chinese	3,063	22%	16,049	28%	424%
Japanese	6,955	49%	11,086	19%	59%
Korean	2,212	16%	17,165	29%	676%
Vietnamese			3,489	6%	n/a
Filipino	1,144	8%	7,059	12%	517%
Hawaiian			253	0.4%	n/a
Other Asian	879	6%	3,205	6%	265%
TOTAL	14,253	100%	58,306	100%	

Source: Survey of Minority Owned Businesses, 1977, 1987

In addition to the sizeable growth in the absolute numbers of firms, the ethnic and industrial composition of Asian business ownership has changed. Most notable is that the Japanese, who comprised nearly a majority in 1977 (49 percent), declined to roughly one-fifth (19 percent) a decade later. Japanese ownership was eclipsed by the dramatic expansion of Chinese and Korean entrepreneurs as both groups garnered roughly 30 percent of Asian business ownership in 1987. Although the rate of Vietnamese business ownership is increasing, it still comprises only a small proportion of Asian firms (6 percent). Filipino business ownership is also quite modest at 12 percent. An industrial recomposition has accompanied the ethnic recomposition. Agricultural firms had made up approximately one in five (19 percent) Asian-owned businesses, but then declined to only 3 percent. Two sectors stand out: retail trade which accounts for slightly over one-quarter, and services which accounts for over two-fifths.

Despite the large number of Asian-owned businesses, this entrepreneurial class has a serious weakness because the typical firm is very small. Three-quarters do not have any paid employees and typically rely on unpaid family labor. The firms with paid employees are typically "very small" businesses with an average of four employees, which is significantly less than the average of 17 for all firms in Los Angeles (Ong and Azores, 1993).

TABLE 2: 1987 Asian Firms in Los Angeles County with Paid Employees

Industry	% w/ emp.	Avg. no. emp.	Avg. payroll
Retail	39%	4.1	$7,807
Service	21%	3.0	12,563
Manufacturing	64%	13.7	7,284
Agriculture	9%	3.9	12,022
Construction	25%	1.5	20,079
Transportation	15%	2.8	15,034
FIRE	7%	2.2	12,479
Wholesale Trade	25%	3.5	17,701
Industries, NC	13%	1.7	14,823
TOTAL AVERAGE	25%	4.2	9,609

Source: Survey of Minority Owned Businesses, 1987

The compensation for paid employees of Asian-owned firms is also quite low. The average annual salary for a worker in an Asian enterprise is $9,609. For those employed in retail trade, which comprises 26 percent of all Asian businesses and is the largest employer next to manufacturing, the average salary is a mere $7,807. Those employed in manufacturing firms fare the worst with an annual salary of $7,284. Workers in service firms, on the other hand, earn $12,563. However, unlike retail and manufacturing firms, only 21 percent of these firms actually employ workers. Moreover, the average number of employees for service firms is three workers compared to four for retail and fourteen for manufacturing (see Table 2).

There are also important wage differences for workers employed by the various Asian ethnic businesses. For the two dominant Asian ethnic business owners, the Chinese and Koreans, annual salaries for their paid employees are lower than the average salary of $9,609 for Asian business employees. Almost one-third (32 percent) of Korean firms have paid employees with an average of 4.4 employees. However, the average annual salary is $8,655. Over one-quarter (28 percent) of Chinese-owned firms have paid employees with an average of 4.8 employees; however, the annual salary is $9,484. It is notable that for the newest Asian entrepreneurial group, the Vietnamese, the average annual wage is a mere $6,119.

Another indicator of the smallness of Asian-owned firms is their modest volume of sales. For the one-quarter (25 percent) of firms with paid employees, the annual sales and receipts is $314,396, which can hardly be considered a huge volume. However, since the majority (75 percent) of Asian businesses do not have paid employees, their average sales and receipts are significantly lower. Table 3 indicates the average annual sales and receipts for Asian firms with no paid employees based on the business owner's ethnicity. Clearly, an overwhelming majority of Asian firms are not only small in size but in revenues as well.

One consequence of the weakness of Asian-owned businesses is a high failure rate. A survey conducted by Bates (1989) shows that for Asian male-owned firms, which formed between 1976 and 1982, the overall rate of business failure by 1986 was 22 percent, with the highest rate of failure for firms with the smallest amount of revenues. Thirty-eight percent of firms that earned between $5,000 and $9,999 failed. For those earning between $10,000 and $24,999, the probability of failure did not improve, as 29 percent failed. Moreover, the chances for business failure appear to vary for Asian ethnic groups, with Indochinese refugees suffering a particularly high rate of failure; for every 20 businesses started by Indochinese refugees each month, 18 failed during the first year (May, 1987).

Ethnic Entrepreneurship as an Economic Strategy

The preceding profile challenges the general public perception that Asians are successful entrepreneurs. Not only are the business conditions of Asian firms less than desirable but the rate of self-employment varies significantly among Asian ethnic groups. While the overall rate of self-employment for Asian men in Los Angeles County is 19 percent, which is only slightly above the Anglo male rate of 18 percent, there are important interethnic differences for Asians. Those with the highest rates of self-employment are Korean men at 38 percent, in contrast to Filipino men at 7 percent (PUMS, 1990). This differential may be an outcome of the different degrees of labor market disadvantage that face these two ethnic groups (Ong and Azores, 1993). Since Filipinos have greater English language abilities than Koreans, they may experience fewer barriers in the mainstream labor market.

TABLE 3: 1987 Average Annual Revenues for Asian-Owned Firms with No Paid Employees By Ethnic Group

	Total Firms	No. Firms w/o emps.	Average Sales and Receipts
Chinese	16,049	11,639	$41,993
Japanese	11,086	8,967	29,517
Korean	17,165	11,660	50,321
Vietnamese	3,489	2,728	28,882
Filipino	7,059	6,110	18,070
Hawaiian	253	216	24,088
Other Asian	3,205	2,322	38,398
TOTAL	58,306	43,642	$37,206

Source: Survey of Minority Owned Businesses, 1987

The factors that contribute to a propensity for self-employment can be generalized according to the interaction of the employment opportunity structure and availability of immigrant resources (Waldinger, 1989). The employment opportunity structure is typically dominated by the continuing presence of high levels of labor market disadvantages, which lead those immigrants with available resources to create alternative employment strategies: namely self-employment opportunities.

Historically, racial discrimination and exclusion from the mainstream labor market helped foster Asian self-employment as an alternative economic strategy. Discrimination also determined the economic activities which Asian entrepreneurs could pursue. Typically, these were activities which served the ethnic community or faced little competition from white entrepreneurs and workers, such as laundries, restaurants, and labor-intensive agriculture. Today, labor market discrimination continues to be a factor in the decision to pursue self-employment. The immigrant propensity toward entrepreneurship is, in part, a response to the lack of employment alternatives and the persistence of labor market barriers such as the lack of English proficiency, devaluation of educational attainment abroad, restrictive licensing requirements, and racial and cultural discrimination (Modell and Bonacich, 1980; Light and Bonacich, 1988; Min, 1984).

One prevalent form of labor market discrimination that has contributed to the emergence of Asian entrepreneurship is the exclusion from white-collar occupations of well-educated Asian immigrants. Their high rate of educational attainment is reflected in the demographic characteristics of Korean business owners; the vast majority were engaged in white-collar and professional occupations prior to immigration to the United States (Min, 1984). Their perception of labor market disadvantages and belief in the advantages of self-employment, particularly the opportunity to recreate job autonomy and economic mobility, contribute to the decision to pursue small business entrepreneurship (Min, 1984). In other words, the inability to find comparable white-collar occupations and subsequent underemployment in the U.S. has led many immigrants to small business ownership.

The finding that Asian entrepreneurs tend to be more educated than other racial groups is substantiated in Bates' study which found that well over one-half (59 percent) of Asian male entrepreneurs have attended four or more years of college compared to 28 percent of African American male entrepreneurs and 35 percent of non-minority male entrepreneurs (Bates, 1989, pp. 32-33). In fact, only a negligible proportion (8 percent) of Asian American male entrepreneurs have less than 12 years of education. Essentially, a primary factor which contributes to Asian small business ownership is the inability of immigrant professionals to locate occupations commensurate with their education and skills. Thus, they turn to small business as an avenue for economic and social mobility. Despite these human capital differences, the total revenues of non-minority male-owned firms ($118,791) continues to exceed that of Asian male-owned firms ($110,952) (Bates, 1989, p. 33).

Structural constraints alone, however, cannot explain the prevalence of Asian-owned businesses. Some immigrant groups develop higher than average rates of business ownership because they have access to ethnic and class resources, or what has been generally described as superior "organizing capacity" -- the ability to mobilize business resources (Kim, Hurh, and Fernandez, 1989; Light, 1984; Light and

Bonacich, 1988). Ethnic and class resources typically differentiate the pre-immigration socioeconomic backgrounds of these immigrants. Ethnic resources include social networks, values, knowledge, informal institutions, and solidarity. Generally, these resources are available to all members of an ethnic group.

In contrast, class resources are available only to a segment of the ethnic group. Class resources are both material, such as property, human capital, personal wealth; and cultural, including bourgeois values and those associated with entrepreneurship (Light, 1984; Light and Bonacich, 1988). Class resources, in particular, material resources, have always been a critical factor in small business start-ups. Among Asian immigrants, Light notes a shift from ethnic to class resources in the formation of small businesses: "Post-1970 Asian immigrants in North America continue to mobilize ethnic resources to support business ownership, but the balance has shifted toward money, human capital, and bourgeois culture" (Light, 1984, p. 76).

Moreover, class culture is reflected in the notion of "status inconsistency," which is a factor that pushes highly educated immigrants to entrepreneurship (Min, 1984). Asians, whose pre-immigration status was in elite occupational and educational categories, when confronted with labor market barriers or "blocked upward mobility" in the United States, will seek self-employment as an avenue to recreate job autonomy, prestige, and personal independence (Min, 1984; Kim, Hurh, and Fernandez, 1989).

The Ethnic Enclave Economy

A large segment of Asian small business development takes place in an ethnic enclave economy where there is access to a cheap immigrant labor force and a market for consumption. Ethnic enclaves often refer to highly visible geographically or spatially bounded economic centers such as Chinatown and Koreatown. Much research on Asian business ownership has been in the context of these ethnic enclaves; however, Asian enterprises are also located in other communities as well, such as Korean merchants in predominantly African American communities. Instead of the notion of ethnic enclave, Light and Bonacich (1988) propose Asian business activity is better conceptualized as an ethnic economy which is not spatially bound but defined largely by the extensive networks of Asian-owned firms, regardless of geographical location.

Based on the literature on ethnic enclaves, agglomeration and vertical and horizontal integration appear to be key factors in defining this enclave. As Light and Bonacich claim, "The concept of ethnic enclave focuses on the development of an institutionally complete ethnic community and its economic base" (Light and Bonacich, 1988, p. xiii). An ethnic economy, on the other hand, is defined as ethnic business owners and their employees, who are often co-ethnics. This concept of an ethnic economy does not require locational clustering of ethnic firms, clientele or cultural ambience within the firm (Light and Bonacich, 1988). While many Asian small businesses are based in an ethnic enclave that is spatially bounded, the broader conceptualization of an ethnic economy permits for a more comprehensive analysis of the status and issues facing Asian small businesses.

More importantly, the literature on ethnic enclaves has centered on a highly contested debate on the impact of participation in the ethnic enclave for immigrant workers. One position argues that the ethnic or kinship bond between employers and employees provides for a mutually beneficial relationship. Common culture and language provide economic benefits to employers based on the reduction of operating costs, recruitment and on-the-job communication costs, as well as a cheaper labor force (Ong, 1984). In exchange for long hours, labor-intensive work, and low wages, employees benefit from a flexible work environment that provides cultural continuity and an internal labor market, as employers are obligated to reserve new opportunities in their businesses for their co-ethnic workers. Employees supposedly receive higher returns for their human capital (skills) than comparable workers in the secondary labor market (Portes and Jensen, 1987; Zhou and Logan, 1991). Moreover, employees may acquire skills that will enable them to pursue self-employment (Bailey and Waldinger, 1992).

Due to these attributes, the ethnic enclave essentially comprises a labor market segment that is "protected," as it shelters participants from outside competition. These qualities have led some scholars to define it as a segment distinct from the primary and secondary labor markets (Wilson and Portes, 1980; Portes and Bach, 1985; Portes and Jensen, 1987). In other words, unlike the secondary labor market, the ethnic enclave offers low-skill immigrant workers opportunities for employment training. Through "training systems," or social networks, the enclaves provide workers with opportunities for skill acquisition and upward mobility and thus, resemble the primary labor market (Bailey and Waldinger, 1992).

In sum, according to ethnic enclave theory, the enclave provides an alternative strategy for the incorporation of immigrants that is distinct from dominant analyses stressing exploitation and assimilation. According to traditional frameworks, immigrants are either channelled into the secondary labor market, where they are subjected to exploitation (Piore, 1979); or start their lives in low-paying jobs but as they gain skills, they assimilate into society and move into jobs, eventually with earnings that exceed that of the native-born (Chiswick, 1980). In contrast, ethnic enclave theory holds that enclaves shelter group members from outside competition, racial discrimination, and government surveillance and regulations (Zhou, 1992). Immigrant entrepreneurs use ethnic solidarity to persuade employees to accept exploitation but, in turn, are bonded to them by mutual obligation (Portes and Bach, 1985).

The key factor in determining economic outcome is not individual skills or ambitions but the social context into which immigrants are received (Portes and Bach, 1985). A central conclusion is that there is no penalty for segregation since enclave workers do better economically than those who accept entry-level jobs in the larger labor market. Unlike secondary labor market workers, enclave workers receive higher returns to human capital (i.e., jobs that more closely correspond with their educational attainment level and earnings commensurate with occupational status) (Portes and Wilson, 1980; Portes and Bach, 1985; Portes and Jensen, 1987; Portes and Jensen, 1989; Zhou, 1992). In other words, "immigrants can succeed without learning English and without joining the American labor market" (Kwong, 1987, p. 6).

Others contend that this conceptualization of an ethnic enclave downplays the exploitative aspects of the employer-employee relationship (Mar, 1991; Light and Bonacich, 1988; Sanders and Nee, 1987). Since the ethnic economy tends to be based on a narrow range of labor intensive industries concentrated in a highly competitive sector of the economy where the potential for the substitution of products or services is extremely high, wages are typically very low, benefits are virtually non-existent, and employment is highly unstable (Ong, 1984). Employer-employee kinship relations may in fact foster an oppressive work environment where workers are expected to submit to harsh conditions. These kinship bonds undermine the possibilities for workers' organizations and channels to air and resolve grievances. Essentially, the isolation of ethnic labor markets from institutions and regulations in the larger society results in the subjection of enclave workers to "the vagaries of the market" (Ong, 1984, p. 37).

In addition to enclave workers, Light and Bonacich (1988) propose that Asian business owners, specifically Koreans, also provide an important source of "cheap labor" to large U.S. firms. Since the majority of Asian-owned businesses are individual proprietorships with few or no employees, most firms rely on the labor of the entrepreneur and unpaid family members. Asian entrepreneurs also assume the risks of inner city investments and provide big firms with indirect access to cheap labor, which permit these firms to avoid the wage and work condition demands of organized labor (Light and Bonacich, 1988, p. 23). Asian entrepreneurs typically undertake business endeavors which are deemed highly undesirable by other entrepreneurs.

Based on these observations, we conclude that Asian ethnic economies -- which include both immigrant business owners and workers -- comprise a segment of the secondary labor market, rather than a distinct labor market segment. In fact, Mar contends that the ethnic labor market comprises a lower tier of the secondary labor market (Mar, 1991, p. 17).

Entrepreneurial Niches

The ethnic economy is distinguished by the concentration of Asian firms in entrepreneurial niches. This phenomenon can be attributed to historical racial discrimination which restricted Asian entrepreneurs to specific economic activities. The creation of these niches is reinforced by the influx of new immigrant entrepreneurs who, faced with limited capital and other barriers, are unable to set up businesses in the more "protected" sectors of the economy. Moreover, social and kinship networks provide new immigrant entrepreneurs with access to a shared collective experience, as well as start-up capital or credit sources, which facilitates the expansion of particular economic niches.

The "low barrier" (i.e., lack of competition) thesis on entrepreneurial niches may partially explain the concentration of Asian small businesses in other minority communities, namely the African American and Latino communities. The markets in these communities are typically underdeveloped due to high crime rates and low-profit margins. The reluctance of firms to set up businesses in these markets creates business opportunities for successive waves of immigrant entrepreneurs (Light and Bonacich, 1988; Waldinger, 1989; Kim, Hurh, and Fernandez, 1989). However, an unfortunate byproduct of this economic reality is heightened racial tensions due to the growing resentment of African Americans and Latinos to the presence of Asian immigrant businesses in their communities.

In sum, Asian immigrants not only face labor market barriers but are also excluded from more profitable retail businesses (Noah, 1991).

As a result, Asian entrepreneurial niches have become known as "business ghettos" (May, 1987). Despite the decades of Asian entrepreneurship in the United States, the bulk of Asian-owned firms can still be described as small endeavors requiring limited start-up capital, concentrated in a few economic niches distinguished by high competition, labor intensiveness, and low profit margins.

Ethnic entrepreneurial niches vary by ethnic groups. In addition to the historically well-known ethnic concentrations such as Chinese restaurants and laundries, and Japanese truck farming, there are new niches such as Korean grocery stores, Thai restaurants, Vietnamese beauty and nail salons, and Cambodian donut shops. A recent article in the *Los Angeles Times* describes the tenuous viability of the donut industry, which is now the source of livelihood for a majority of Cambodian small business owners (Akst, 1993). According to Vora H. Kanthoul of the Cambodian Business Association, approximately 80 percent of Cambodian business owners are donut shop owners (Akst, 1993). These small shops survive due to hard work and unpaid family labor. Typically, the husbands bake all night and the wives and children work the counter during the day. The overall decline in Southern California's economy has eroded much of the foot traffic which serves as the economic mainstay for small donut shops. As a result, Cambodian business owners are struggling, and find that to remain competitive requires even more sacrifices.

TABLE 4: Industrial Concentration of Asian-Owned Businesses by Ethnicity

	Service	Retail	FIRE	Whls.	Const.	Manf.
Chinese	42%	29%	10%	4%	4%	3%
Japanese	49%	17%	8%	3%	4%	3%
Korean	41%	38%	4%	3%	5%	3%
Vietnam	41%	26%	4%	1%	3%	8%
Filipino	54%	15%	13%	2%	4%	2%

Source: Survey of Minority Owned Businesses, 1987

A review of the broad industrial sectors of Asian business ownership by ethnicity reflects some differences in areas of ethnic concentration. Although the Survey of Minority Owned Businesses data on industry by ethnicity was only available on a national level and the industrial categories are admittedly quite broad, the statistics do reflect some important distinctions for Asian ethnic groups (see Table 4).

While the two dominant sectors of Asian business ownership are services and retail trade, there are some notable ethnic differences. There is a higher proportion of Filipinos in service and FIRE firms than other sectors. Among the ethnic groups least represented in FIRE firms are Koreans and Vietnamese. Interestingly, both Japanese and Vietnamese entrepreneurs are represented among agricultural, forestry and fishing businesses. Koreans are concentrated in service and retail businesses. Vietnamese are least represented in wholesale trade, and a notable share of Vietnamese businesses are in manufacturing. Overall, approximately one in five (21 percent) Asian-owned business nationwide is either a food store or an eating and drinking place.

Employment Conditions in the Ethnic Economy

Ethnic enterprises serve a central role in the labor market incorporation of Asian immigrants who are largely excluded from the mainstream labor market. For a number of reasons, ethnic business owners prefer to hire co-ethnics (Waldinger, 1986). Our survey (SALIC, 1993) confirms that a sizeable portion of Asian immigrant workers are employed by co-ethnics in small enterprises; 40 percent of workers are employed in the ethnic economy. On average, 70 percent of the workforce in these businesses are of the same ethnicity as the survey respondent. These businesses are typically small retail operations, restaurants, and garment shops located within low-income ethnic communities where the workers live. Fifty-six percent of workers in the ethnic economy report that their place of employment is within five miles of their homes, compared to only 22 percent of workers outside the ethnic economy.

As expected, workers are drawn to the ethnic economy in part because of limited English proficiency. Among survey respondents, two-thirds (66 percent) of workers in the ethnic economy speak English "not at all" or "not well," compared with only 20 percent of workers outside the ethnic economy. Although small businesses have been long recognized and lauded as an important source of job creation, many of the jobs generated pay low wages and have low skills. The median wage of workers in the ethnic economy is $5.25 per hour, only 60 percent of the $8.75 median wage of workers outside the ethnic economy (SALIC, 1993). Not surprisingly, when compared to Asian entrepreneurs, the earnings of workers in ethnic economies are significantly lower. For example, among the Chinese (both from China and Taiwan) in the Los Angeles metropolitan region, the mean income of the self-employed was $20,151, compared to wage workers whose mean income was $11,994 (Razin, 1989, p. 293). A comparable income disparity was evident for the Korean self-employed whose mean income was $20,259, while wage workers earned $12,122.

Based on an estimate of average yearly wages for employees of Asian-owned firms from the 1987 Survey of Minority Owned Business Enterprises, the earnings of workers were considerably lower than that reported in the Razin (1989) article. This earnings disparity appears to dispute the claim that workers in the ethnic economy receive a higher return to their human capital than wage workers employed in other sectors of the economy. By dividing the annual payroll by the number of paid employees, the mean annual salaries for employees in Vietnamese-, Korean-, and Chinese-owned firms were among the lowest at $6119, $8655, and $9484 respectively. Along with low wages and poor working conditions, employees of small businesses also lack health insurance coverage. SALIC (1993) results show that only 26 percent of workers in the ethnic economy have medical coverage, while twice as many workers outside of the ethnic economy, 54 percent, have coverage.

Conclusion: Focus on Low-Income Asians in the Ethnic Economy

Despite the prevalence of small competitive firms, low profit margins, and labor intensive production processes, the Asian ethnic economy undoubtedly provides a crucial source of employment for immigrant workers. The vitality of this economic segment, however, is dependent on the exploitation of immigrant workers who typically have no other employment options. In light of the high rate of failure for small businesses, and the saturation of the ethnic market, it is highly unlikely that many enclave participants will find opportunities for upward mobility, contrary to the analyses from the ethnic enclave thesis.

While workers in the ethnic economy can be viewed as the "exploited of the exploited," immigrant entrepreneurs also pay a high economic and social-psychological price for self-employment (Kim, Hurh, and Fernandez, 1989). In addition to long working hours, physical and financial risks, and other problems of operating a small business, entrepreneurs also bear such "social costs" as domestic violence, child neglect, divorce, and family breakdown (Bonacich, 1988). According to Molly Huynh, student author of one of our case studies on a family-owned business:

> [S]mall business, while seeming to be the answer and the key to success, often turns out to have great detrimental consequences to the Asian family and the workplace dynamics. The dream of having a constant source of income often means that each family member must not only contribute their time and energy, but must also be willing to change lifestyles or career plans "for the good of the family business." This sacrificial mentality is so common and prevalent that it has become the norm and the hallmark of the Asian-owned family business.

In summary, although Asians appear to have created their own solution to labor market barriers through small business development, it is necessary to recognize the dual nature of the ethnic economy as both a flourishing center and a source of tremendous hardship and exploitation. It is critical to recognize that ethnic ties among employers and employees can promote self-help but they can also depoliticize the employer-worker relationship and undermine worker rights (Bonacich, 1980; Ong, 1984; Light and Bonacich, 1988). Moreover, the higher returns to human capital for ethnic enclave workers remain questionable, and opportunities for training and mobility are not as prevalent as proponents of the ethnic enclave theory believe, evidenced by the many immigrant workers trapped in low wage, low skill jobs.

Finally, the focus on the benefits of the ethnic economy shifts public policy attention away from persistent labor market discrimination and growing lack of employment faced by many Asian immigrants in the mainstream economy. Historically, self-employment was the only alternative to joblessness for Asian immigrants. Today, many Asians continue to seek their economic livelihood through risky and labor-intensive self-employment endeavors. Moreover, for immigrant workers facing serious labor market barriers, employment in the ethnic economy is often their only strategy for economic survival.

PART II

RETHINKING POLICIES

CHAPTER FIVE

Job Training and Workers' Rights

This chapter focuses on policies and programs aimed at correcting the problems of joblessness and low-wage employment. More than any single factor, the type of employment held by individuals determines their well-being and, in turn, the overall characteristic of the community. Despite the relatively high number of entrepreneurs documented in the previous chapters, the vast majority of Asian Americans in low-income neighborhoods make a living as paid laborers. Even for households where the adults are not employed, wage work is the most feasible avenue to self sufficiency. Earning a decent wage is necessary to have decent shelter, adequate food and the normal pleasures of life that most of us take for granted.

Gainful employment is not only a financial necessity but also the prevailing social norm. This is certainly true for the larger society, which values the "virtue of work." As David Ellwood, a leading analyst on poverty in the United States, notes:

> The work ethic is fundamental to our conceptions of ourselves and our expectations of others. People ought to work hard not only to provide for their families, but because laziness and idleness are seen as indications of weak moral character. The idle rich command as much disdain as jealousy; the idle poor are scorned. (1988, p. 16)

Asian Americans also place a high value on work. The attitudes in San Francisco Chinatown are representative, where the typical resident works in order to avoid "tarnishing his public image and, perhaps more important, to avoid bringing shame upon the family" (Ong, 1984, p. 50). Even among those collecting public assistance, there is a strong drive to work. One survey found that over two-thirds of Asian respondents had attempted to exit welfare, a considerably higher proportion than that for other racial groups (Hasenfeld, 1991).

Unfortunately, finding meaningful employment is an elusive dream for many. While some of the poor are jobless, there is also a large number of "working poor" in the United States (Gardner and Herz, 1992). In Los Angeles County, the ranks of the jobless and the working poor have grown dramatically over the last two decades (Ong et al., 1989). Asian Americans are a part of this unfortunate trend. Among the working class, about a quarter are found in the most disadvantaged jobs (Toji and Johnson, 1992, p. 85). Many of these individuals work full-time, year-round but are still poor. Moreover, working conditions are often deplorable, unhealthy, and unsafe. Among the jobless, the individuals facing innumerable problems are those dependent on public assistance. As we stated earlier, up to half of the Cambodians in Long Beach rely on AFDC (Aid to Families with Dependent Children).

The employment-related problems faced by both the working poor and the jobless must be addressed by the following principles of Community Economic Development:

- Everyone should have an opportunity for employment;
- Workers are entitled to a decent wage;
- Workers should be protected from unfair labor practices;
- For the able-bodied on welfare, public assistance should be transitional, a stepping stone toward full employment.

Although these goals are widely accepted, we are a long way from achieving them. Several factors, most of which are discussed in earlier chapters, contribute to low-income Asian Americans being disadvantaged in the labor market and exploited at the work place. These include: difficulties with the English language, too few marketable skills, little understanding of how the American labor market functions, and a lack of understanding of their legal rights. Overcoming these deficiencies can give low-income Asian Americans greater access to better employment.

This chapter examines two employment-related policies that have potential relevance for low-income Asians. The first is government supported job training, which can improve the skills of workers, thus enabling the jobless to obtain work and low-wage workers to find higher-paying jobs. SALIC reveals the potential benefits of job training: a male Chinese respondent from Long Beach was able to advance from unemployment to a $12 an hour job as a machinist after completing a job training program.

The second policy area is workers' legal rights. California has numerous labor laws designed to protect employees, and by exercising these rights, workers are less likely be exploited. For Asian communities and residents to take full advantage of existing training programs and labor laws, community-based organizations (CBOs) must become more involved in employment-related programs.

Job Training Policies and Programs

Manpower policies, the broader category that covers employment-related issues, date back to the First World War, but efforts to assist low-income and minority populations emerged in the early 1960s as a key element of the War on Poverty (Ulman, 1974, p. 87). Job training was seen as a major component in helping adults (and youth) escape poverty. Over the last three decades, the federal government, which provides the bulk of the funds in this field, has enacted several employment acts. Today, there are three major programs related to job training for disadvantaged workers: the Job Training Partnership Act (JTPA), Greater Avenues for Independence (GAIN), and Targeted Jobs Tax Credit (TJTC). Another program of interest is the Targeted Assistance Program (TAP), which is aimed at refugees on welfare.

JTPA (Job Training Partnership Act), established in 1982, is the federal government's primary employment program, and its primary purpose is "to afford job training to those economically disadvantaged individuals and other individuals facing serious barriers to employment, who are in special need of such training to obtain productive employment." The enactment of JTPA signaled a major switch in policy by the federal government away from direct job-creation in the public sector, which had been the core of CETA (Comprehensive Employment and Training Act), during the 1970s (Levitan and Gallo, 1992). With JTPA, the emphasis shifted to securing jobs in the private sector through a cooperative partnership between government and the private sector.

Under JTPA, the local agency for each Service Delivery Area (SDA) makes decisions on allocating the funds. This region has eight SDAs, including Los Angeles County and the cities of Los Angeles and Long Beach. The Private Industry Council, where representatives from the private sector form a majority, formulates policy guidelines and provides general oversight. A network of firms and community-based organizations provide the actual job training and employment services to participants. Participants received classroom training, ESL instruction, and subsidized on-the-job training for entry-level positions in such trades as clerical and secretarial work, bank teller, hotel industry worker, and data entry. Job placement, work experience, and employment support services are also provided.

GAIN (Greater Avenues for Independence), the second major job training, is a California initiative designed to reduce welfare usage by improving the education and job skills of its participants. This program is one of numerous welfare reforms since the early 1980s. WIN, a work incentive program that focused on job search and subsidized work experience, was the most widely adopted approach, and required recipients with no children under the age of six to search for work, often with little training. GAIN, which started in San Diego County, represents this state's current effort under the national Job Opportunities and Basic Skills Training (JOBS) Program. Those eligible to participate in GAIN include welfare-dependent single heads of a household (primarily women) with children of school age and heads of a two-parent family (usually men).

The program provides a set of employment-related services including basic education, ESL instruction, on-the-job training, vocational training, support services such as job search assistance and adult school. Where appropriate, GAIN subsidizes tuition, transportation (gas or fare), child care and purchase of textbooks. Training is provided through a number of sources: community colleges, adult schools, regional occupational centers, child care agencies, Job Training Partnership Act (JTPA) programs and local unemployment offices. Participants may stay in these programs for as long as needed to advance to the next level of training. Programs at vocational schools for specific job training is a two-year option. If one has already taken two years of community college, GAIN may pay for two more years of community college education. GAIN does not pay for a four-year college education. In job training, GAIN gives priority to occupations that have the best chance of offering employment that will not become obsolete, such as secretarial and clerical work, computer operator, medical assistant, nurses aid and medical technologist.

Each county determines the mix of services offered and the target population according to its priorities, local economic needs and employment opportunities, and the particular characteristics and composition of its welfare recipients. Los Angeles County registers only recipients who have been on public assistance for at least three consecutive years, and has a disproportionate number of individuals taking part in basic educational training such as ESL (English as a Second Language) training, GED (General Educational Development) preparation for those without a high school education, and Adult Basic Education.

In addition to GAIN, TAP (Targeted Assistance Program) provides help to Asian refugees on welfare. Priority is given to those who have been in the country for 36 months or less, those who are school dropouts, and those with poor or no command of English. The program provides job training services, ESL instruction, skills training, and support services for refugees who are at or below the poverty income level with the goal of promoting self-sufficiency by increasing their potential for achieving gainful un-subsidized employment.

Unlike JTPA and GAIN, which provide mechanisms for direct involvement by local government and CBOs, TJTC (Targeted Jobs Tax Credit) works through the federal tax system and gives tax credit to employers who hire and retain disadvantaged individuals, including low-income youths and welfare recipients. The purpose of this program is to induce private firms to provide work experience by lowering labor costs. The government subsidizes 40 percent of the first year's wages, up to a maximum tax credit of $2,400 per employee. In exchange, employers are required to keep the worker for at least 90 days or 120 hours. The maximum credit and minimum work requirement for summer youth employment are lower. There are no provisions for training, although it is possible for participants to acquire some on-the-job skills.

Limitations of Job-Training

Despite the promise of a high return to public investments in human capital for the disadvantaged, job training programs suffer from severe limitations. First, the programs often "cream," or choose the most marketable applicants and eliminate those with the greatest needs. Second, the outcomes for participants are marginal, with most job placements in low-wage, entry positions. And third, limited funding has meant only a small proportion of the needy is served.

Like many social service programs, job training programs cream because service providers must meet performance standards. Although per capita cost is no longer used as a criterion, providers are still judged by the post-training employment rates and earnings of participants (U.S. GAO, 1993; California, Employment Development Department, 1993, pp. 3-4) Under these conditions "contractors have a strong incentive for screening applicants in order to serve those who have the most skills, most education, and can be trained most quickly and at least cost -- in short, the most employable" (Romero and Gonzales, 1989, p. 15). Unfortunately, this creates a bias against the hard-to-serve clients such as individuals with little or no employment skills, or limited English proficiency. One adverse consequence is that minorities, including Asians, are often underserved because they are high-risk participants (U.S. GAO, 1991b).

Even with the tendency to select low-risk participants, outcomes are less than spectacular. Not all enrollees finish the program, and among those who do, not all are placed in jobs. In the Los Angeles SDA, the adult placement rate for those who complete training is only 63 percent, and the average hourly wage of adult participants who had previous wages only improved from $6.34 prior to entering the program to $6.82 after completing training. The approximate half-dollar increase translates to a 7.5 percent increase, which is probably better than what a worker would have experienced without the training but is nonetheless small. Consequently, the minimal improvement is insufficient to significantly upgrade the quality of life of the working poor.

The performance of TJTC (Targeted Jobs Tax Credit) is equally poor. The overwhelming majority of the jobs it corrects are low-wage positions in services, clerical work, and sales (U.S. GAO, 1991a). Over two-thirds of the workers in 1988 made $4.00 or less, and post-placement turnovers were very high. TJTC workers did experience increased earnings, particularly among those without any prior work experience, but the increase "may be more related to the general transition to the work force than to their participation in the TJTC program" (U.S. GAO, 1991a, p. 25). Although there are no data for Los Angeles, we suspect that the same conclusions apply to this region.

Improvements for welfare recipients are also minimal. An analysis of the second-year results in Los Angeles indicates that GAIN increased earnings and lowered welfare payments (Friedlander et al., 1993). Nonetheless, not all found work, and the jobs that were filled were primarily low-wage ones. GAIN participants had a higher employment rate than non-GAIN recipients, but nonetheless, less than a quarter of the former group had some employment during the second year. Those who did work had low-wage jobs. According to JTPA participant statistics for the Los Angeles SDA, the post-JTPA average hourly wage of all adult participants on welfare before the program is $6.98. The same can be said of GAIN in general because participants who reach the point of seeking employment likely find a job that does not remove them from poverty. For TAP, hourly wage information provided by several different Asian service providers suggests that post-training average wages are also low, ranging from $5.00 - $6.00 per hour.

Of course, moving from welfare dependency to unsubsidized employment is an improvement, and given the low skills of many of the participants, this can be considered an accomplishment. Yet, many of these individuals simply have joined the ranks of the working poor. Job training helps people into entry-level jobs but without additional training, many will remain stuck in low quality, low-wage jobs. At best, the promise of becoming a productive member of society is only partially fulfilled.

Even if we disregard creaming and marginal outcomes, job training programs have another major flaw. They fail to reach a significant number of individuals and to provide continuous upgrading of skills because funding has declined while needs have increased due to the growth of people in poverty and workers in low-wage jobs. Between 1979 and 1984, for example, per capita funding in real dollars for the Department of Labor for employment and training programs was cut by over three-quarters (Bassi and Ashenfelter, 1986, p. 137). This decline was part of a broader withdrawal by the Republican administration from efforts to address of poverty in the U.S. (Katz, 1986; Skocpol, 1991).

The tax incentives (credits) to the private sector have not offset the decline in program funding. The total credits claimed over a ten-year period, which includes most of the 1980s, amounted to less than half of the current annual budget for job training for the economically disadvantaged (U.S. GAO, 1991a; U.S. GAO, 1993). The program reaches only a small proportion of the eligible participants (Levitan and Gallo, 1987). Moreover, less than half of the firms receiving credits made specific efforts to recruit and hire targeted groups, indicating that most of the hiring would have occurred even without the subsidy (U.S. GAO, 1991a).

The above limitations of job training apply to all poor people, but Asian Americans face additional problems and barriers associated with their particular needs. For example, the application process for job training programs is particularly difficult for immigrants. Several representatives from Asian service providers of JTPA training remarked that many who are eligible do not enroll because they lack the proper documentation which includes such things as income information for the last 6 months, verification of residency, and birth certificate (Ng, 1993; Chun, 1993). Some prospective participants lose interest in the program when they realize how difficult it is to apply (Hernandez, 1993).

Moreover, the appropriate training is not always provided. The ESL component of these job training programs is often insufficient to meet the needs of Asian participants. Learning a new language is a difficult task, particularly for Asian immigrants and refugees, who arrive with little schooling. Yet the ESL instruction that is part of these job training programs usually lasts only several weeks or a few months, which is far too short for participants to learn English adequately. Consequently, it is not surprising that programs frequently have trouble placing participants in jobs requiring basic English language training.

Among those who do participate in a training program, the effectiveness of training varies considerably across Asian sub-populations (Chun, 1993; Wing, 1993). Younger females benefit most, in part because they have the opportunity for more extended training and because employers are more willing to hire them for entry-level jobs that also offer opportunities for upward mobility. Interestingly, this outcome holds not only for younger Asian females but also for females in general (Bassi and Ashenfelter, 1986). On the other hand, older Asian males, who tend to be the primary earners in a household and can spare little time for extended training, tend to derive little benefits from job training. In light of the performance standards tied to job-training funding, these variations can create subtle pressure on providers to bypass those with the greatest needs, and this pressure is likely to apply equally to Asian CBOs because they operate under the same reward system (Sy, 1993).

The problem of inadequate training is rooted in inadequate funding. This occurs at two levels. The first is an inadequate share of the existing resources. In the fight for limited job-training resources, Asian organizations have fared poorly because they do not have the political power to gain a fair share (Wing, 1993). Of course, Asian Americans can also be served by non-Asian providers, but even taking this into account, Asian Americans appear to be underserved. For example, Asians comprised over a tenth of the poverty population in California in 1990, but comprised only 8 percent of the 1991-92 state-wide participants in JTPA Title IIA programs. Despite this disparity, our sense is that Asian Americans have and will make significant progress in receiving a fair share of the existing resources.

A far greater problem is the inadequate aggregate resources going to all job training programs for the disadvantaged. With public funding severely limited, Asian CBOs are forced to compete against other communities for very scarce resources. Consequently, it is not surprising that only a small fraction of the SALIC respondents have received any job training. The inadequate investment in people is not only a tragedy for individuals, but also a net loss for society because not all members can reach their potential.

Workers' Rights

The next policy area is the labor laws that govern employment. While job training programs are designed to help individuals improve their skills so they can find employment or find better jobs, labor laws are designed to ensure fair labor practices. In California, these laws determine wages, working conditions and what is expected from the employee and employer relationship. All industries are required to abide by the minimum requirements of the labor standards, Title 8, Code of Regulations. Some of the most important laws are:

- A minimum wage of $4.25 per hour;
- Overtime pay equivalent to one-and-one-half the regular pay must be paid for all hours worked over eight in one day and double the rate of pay for all hours worked over 12 in one day;
- For each hour worked over 40 hours in a week, one-and-one-half the regular rate of pay must be paid;
- In industries that use piecework, earnings must equal or exceed the minimum wage and overtime for the hours worked;
- An itemized statement of deductions must be given to each worker with each payment of wages;
- If an employee quits without notice, the wages are due and payable no later that 72 hours later. If an employee is discharged, all wages earned by an employee are due immediately;
- If an employee is scheduled to report for work and does report but is given less than half the scheduled day's work, the employee must be paid one-half of the

scheduled day's work. If the employee is not put to work, he or she must be paid at least two hours wages;

- A rest period of least ten minutes must be provided for each four hours worked. Meal periods of at least 30 minutes must be provided for each five hours of work;
- Employers must carry a policy of Worker's Compensation Insurance covering all employees;
- Employers must provide training and instruction to all employees when a new work procedure or equipment is first implemented; and
- Supervisors are to familiarize employees with the safety and health hazards, and instruct employees in general safe work practices.

Violation of a labor law can result in a fine against the employer as well as restitution to the worker. For some infractions concerning health and safety, employers can be cited and given a fine up to $7,000. When an accident causes a severe injury or death, jail sentence can be imposed on top of a fine.

California's Division of Labor Standards Enforcement in the Department of Industrial Relations is responsible for enforcing wage and work-hour rules. The Bureau of Field Enforcement, which has an office in Los Angeles, is responsible for investigating violations. Investigations can be initiated by outside complaints and by the Bureau. Moreover, the Division is responsible for producing a plan giving enforcement priorities to areas where workers are relatively low-paid and unskilled, and in industries where there has been a history of violations, such as garment manufacturing, hotels and restaurants, and fast food outlets. This type of enforcement takes the form of a "sweep," where a team of inspectors looks for violations in a given industry for a well defined geographic area.

California's Occupational Safety and Health Administration (OSHA) is responsible for enforcing the state health and safety provisions. Priority is giving to tracking industries with high rates of infractions. Inspectors periodically inspect firms in these industries for toxic or hazardous materials or other harmful conditions to humans or the environment. OSHA also enforces the state provisions related to industrial accidents. The agency requires an employer to report an on-the-job accident, and it is standard practice for OSHA to send an inspector to examine the work site.

Despite the extensive set of labor codes, many employers still treat their workers unfairly, forcing them to accept subminimal wages and to work under unsafe conditions. These practices exist, in part, because many individuals do not know their rights and their entitlement concerning employment, but the problem is more systemic.

Limitations of Workers' Rights

Although labor codes are designed to assist and serve people employed in California, many of the laws and their enforcement are problematic. A general complaint is that labor laws are too complicated for the common man and woman to understand. These laws are written in legal terminology and intended for a highly educated audience. For someone who is uneducated and cannot read or understand English, these laws are incomprehensible. Some specific laws are ambiguous and vague. For example, category 15 on Temperature states that "the temperature maintained in each work area shall provide reasonable comfort consistent with industry-wide standards for the nature of the process and the work performed."

Enforcement is problematic because government agencies are understaffed, with too few field inspectors to effectively and efficiently carry out the responsibilities and duties of the state agencies. Due to limited budgets, field inspectors cannot patrol all of the relevant industries or businesses for potential violations. Rather, state enforcement agencies rely heavily on complaints from workers or third-party monitoring groups, which is the most common procedure of initiating investigations of employers for potential infractions of labor laws (California, Division of Labor Standards Enforcement, 1989). This approach, however, depends on workers' initiative.

Unfortunately, filing a complaint is not easy. To initiate a complaint, one needs to find the right agency, and then locate the right staff person. Some agencies make callers go through a long automated tape before they are allowed to speak to a person. Even for those individuals who exercise their rights, they can become entangled in a cumbersome process. It can take up to several weeks before a complaint is processed through the bureaucracy. According to an inspector from the Division of Labor, Labor Standards Enforcement, many of these delays are a response to Californians being "sue-happy," that is, being litigious. It is asserted that the red-tape is needed if the agency should be taken to court, but it is likely that the process is time consuming for other factors. Regardless of the reason, the end result is a system that discourages workers from exercising their rights and allows many violators to evade labor laws.

Although Asian American workers suffer from numerous unfair labor practices, they face additional barriers to exercising their rights. As stated earlier, low-income Asian Americans are concentrated in the secondary sector of the labor market, where infraction of labor law is prevalent. Many work in the ethnic sub-economy, where employers are under tremendous competitive pressure to cut labor costs, often by using unfair labor practices. Although there is no reliable statistics on the relative incidents of violations in this sub-economy, one labor-law expert states that infractions are much more frequent in the ethnic sector than in the rest of the economy (Wong, 1993). The problems include subminimal wages, demanding kick-backs from tips, extremely low piece rates, and under-the-table payments.

An example of poor working conditions can be found in the garment industry, which employs a large number of low-income Asian Americans (Kim, Nakamura, Fong, Cabarloc, Jung, and Lee, 1992, p.72). Shops in Los Angeles and Long Beach operate in dirty, decrepit buildings which usually have no heating or air conditioning. Some factories in Long Beach (and Orange County) are located in business parks or garage-like warehouses with little ventilation. Even with fans, the rooms are stifling and unbearable in the summer. Meanwhile, many manufacturers, who remain at legal arms length from the exploitative conditions through a system of subcontracting, have showrooms in plush, high-rise offices in the California Market.

Despite the blatant violations, Asian workers frequently have no recourse. Along with being understaffed, enforcement agencies have few bilingual inspectors (Wong, 1993). The system of worker initiated complaints breaks down because many Asian workers are kept in the dark about their rights. By law, the "Official Notice" stating the labor laws is required to be in plain view so employees can read them to inform themselves of their rights. In some cases, employers of Asian workers post the "Official Notice," as required by law, but these notices are written in English only (Kim, Nakamura, Fong, Cabarloc, Jung, and Lee, 1992). This posting fulfills the legal requirement but nonetheless defeats the purpose of informing employees of their rights when the workers cannot read English. There are efforts to overcome this. Some agencies have translated flyers and pamphlets into Spanish, Vietnamese, Chinese, Malaysian and Korean. Large-scale production and wide distribution of such material are necessary steps in educating Asian employers and workers, but the dissemination of information alone is insufficient.

When low-income Asian Americans attempt to report a violation, they are confronted with complicated and confusing bureaucratic process. As stated before, filing a complaint is a disconcerting experience even for a person who is educated and speaks English. For workers who only speak an Asian language or have a poor command of the English language, the process is an even more frustrating and intimidating.

> Imagine trying to collect back wages by seeking the help of a government agency. At the agency's office, you are intimidated by the indifference of the government representative who is impatient with your inability to speak English. All the brochures and forms are in English. Once the forms are completed, you fall through the cracks and cannot get help because there is not enough staff to handle your case. (Lee, 1992, p. 97).

There are only a few Asian translators, who mainly speak Chinese or Vietnamese; consequently, many with limited English ability have faced a nearly insurmountable barrier in filing a complaint.

Beyond the inadequate information and limited bilingual service is a more fundamental problem. Many fear losing their job if they complain to an official government agency:

> If the complainant still works for the company and the boss finds out that you tried to stand up for rights, you will get fired. Learning about rights and actively exercising them can have dangerous implications. (Lee, 1992, p. 97)

The types of employment available to low-income Asian Americans are already unstable, and for some, having a bad job is better than having no job. Because the weakness in the enforcement system and the lack of viable employment opportunities, employers often can use unfair labor practices with impunity at the expense of workers.

The Role of CBOs

Many of the problems and limitations of job training and workers' rights can only be addressed by the state or federal governments, but CBOs can nonetheless play an important role in helping low-income Asian Americans workers. Given the ethnic and cultural nature of the specific issues facing this group, Asian CBOs with their bilingual/bicultural staff and location within the community are in a unique position to be direct providers of training and information, and to be advocates for these workers. Compared to state agencies, CBOs are less intimidating for recent immigrants and refugees.

In the area of disseminating information, CBOs should be a clearinghouse on training opportunities, tax credits, labor laws, and safety and health regulations. CBOs should increase their efforts to refer eligible individuals to job training and education classes available through nearby schools and other agencies. Employers should be given information on the Targeted Jobs Tax Credit discussed earlier. Interviews with Asian American CBOs show no concerted effort to encourage wider usage of TJTC subsidies by firms. At the same time, low-wage workers need to know that they may be entitled to the Earned Income Tax Credit (EIC), which provides a refundable tax credit to working parents with modest incomes (Hoffman, 1990, p.7). In the area of workers' rights, CBOs can distribute translated pamphlets to both employers and employees, and can assist government agencies such as Cal/OSHA and other enforcement agencies by sponsoring workshops on workers rights.

CBOs should help workers who want to form labor unions or coalitions to improve working conditions, wages or benefits. The founding of the national Asian Pacific American Labor Alliance in 1992 has improved Asian American participation in the U.S. labor movement, but more grass-roots organizing is needed. A model of community-based labor organizing is the Korean Immigrant Workers Advocates (KIWA), which seeks to empower and educate Korean immigrant workers on basic workers' rights through education, the provision of related services, advocacy, and organizing.

CBOs should expand their provision of job training within their respective communities. Some Asian CBOs have been involved in job training for over a decade (Aguilar, 1993), but the demand for this service has grown dramatically with the new immigration. Where appropriate, job training should be integrated with the broad programmatic efforts discussed in the other two chapters in this section of the book -- small business development and construction of affordable housing. This integration would increase the effectiveness of the individual programs. An example of this is Asian Neighborhood Design in San Francisco, where workers are trained in construction skills through projects that produce furniture and housing for the community. Similarly, CBOs can combine programs that improve the viability of small Asian-owned businesses and train workers, while using tax credit to cover some of the costs.

Finally, CBOs must act as advocates. This is done by assisting individuals who are having difficulties securing assistance from existing governmental agencies. The role of advocate, however, is broader than this ombudsman-type activity. Because CBOs are in a position to witness the weaknesses in job training programs and the enforcement of labor laws, they should take on the responsibility of informing government administrators of the deficiencies. For example, they should play a role in helping agencies set priorities for funding and for investigation and enforcement.

Recommendations and Strategies

Activities at the community level must be complemented by efforts to change national and state policies. Specifically:

1. The needs and concerns of low-income people, including low-income Asian Americans, must be integrated into the current effort by the U.S. Department of Labor to formulate a new manpower agenda to meet the challenges of an integrated global economy. We applaud the concept of continuous upgrading of skills, which is designed to increase worker productivity and keep the United States competitive. When this approach is applied to disadvantaged populations, it provides an avenue of continuous upward mobility.

2. There must be a broader view of the function of job training. We accept the concept of job training as an investment to increase the productivity of workers based on an economic-efficiency criterion. However, the returns must also be seen in social terms. All people should be given an opportunity to become productive citizens. Job training programs must include a component that enables providers to work with high-risk individuals.

3. Programs that provide economic incentives for the private sector to hire the disadvantaged must be

revised so more of those trapped in low-wage jobs are eligible. To prevent potential abuses of tax credits, there must be training requirements for firms receiving subsidies.

4. Welfare policies should provide greater incentives and support for those who can work. We must dismantle the system where working is economically an undesirable choice for many low-income adults. This should be done not by penalizing the poor but by giving greater assistance to the working poor. This includes larger refunds through the Earned Income Tax Credits so that these workers can have a decent standard of living.

5. The institutional framework to ensure that workers are protected from unfair labor practices must be rebuilt. The national and state agencies that oversee the enforcement of labor laws were seriously weakened during the 1980s. There is now an opportunity to strengthen these institutions, but in doing so, we must insist that they provide equal access to all workers, regardless of ethnicity.

CHAPTER SIX

Alternative Business Development

Self-employment continues to be an important cornerstone of Asian economic activity. Historically, discrimination barred early immigrants from mainstream jobs, forcing many into ethnic entrepreneurship. Today, small businesses remain an important alternative to employment in the mainstream labor market, as Asians continue to face barriers such as discrimination, lack of English language proficiency and transferable skills, and underemployment. Moreover, the belief that self-employment is a superior alternative to low-wage work as a strategy for upward mobility has historical salience for both immigrants and native-born alike.

Although Asian businesses are a vital economic activity, we need to examine the general characteristics of these businesses as well as qualitative issues such as the nature of jobs they create, the diversity of business activities, and their long-term viability. As discussed in Chapter Four, the level of entrepreneurial spirit in the Asian community has historically been high due to the class and ethnic resources of some immigrants. Rather than uncritically promote new business start-ups, it is now both timely and necessary to focus on ways to improve the conditions of existing businesses and the welfare of their workers.

The factors that shape the characteristics of Asian entrepreneurship force many businesses into highly competitive and marginal economic sectors which contribute to exploitative working conditions. Our chief concern is the extent that immigrant entrepreneurs and their businesses can play in improving the quality of community life through jobs with better pay and benefits, services that enrich the business climate, and strategies that diversify the community's economic base.

The Potentials and Limits of Small Business

Small business development is a vital part of national and local economic activity. Within the past two decades, important economic trends have helped to facilitate the expansion and growing significance of small businesses in the United States. The Small Business Administration (SBA) defines a small business as a firm with fewer than 500 employees. Small businesses constitute 99.8 percent of all firms in the United States (Schindler, 1992), but many of these firms do not have employees. In 1986, of the 17 million businesses filing federal tax returns, slightly over three-quarters (76 percent), or 13 million, had no employees (Blackford, 1991, p. 107). The SBA claims that the estimated 20 million small businesses in the United States today accounts for 39 percent of the GNP, one-half of America's workforce, and 54 percent of all sales (SBA, 1992).

The economic restructuring of the 1970s and 1980s, and, specifically, the emergence of an integrated global economy has undermined the viability of many large American businesses, especially in manufacturing. This trend of deindustrialization and the shift from large manufacturing companies to service-related businesses has contributed to the growth of small businesses (Piore, 1990). Numerous large corporations have undertaken drastic measures to downsize their labor force, marking the decline of monopoly capitalism. As big businesses have ceased to be the primary "engines of growth," some policy-makers believe that small firms can serve an important role in economic restructuring and become a vital source of economic revitalization and employment (Mokry, 1988; Blackford, 1991). Current economic conditions of instability favor the emergence of small businesses, since they "have greater ability to react quickly to alterations in markets and fluctuations in exchange rates" (Blackford, 1991, p. 110).

Exactly how important small businesses are to economic development is, however, unclear. David Birch's (1987) seminal study claims that two-thirds (66 percent) of the new jobs created between 1969 and 1976 were by companies that employed fewer than 20 workers. This assertion is highly disputed, and many economists argue for a different figure (see Piore, 1990, for a summary). Some contend that firms employing fewer than 20 employees are responsible for a little over one-third (37 percent) of new jobs. Between 1985-1986, firms with fewer than 100 employees accounted for 44 percent of new jobs in the United States (Blackford, 1991, p. 115).

Even if small businesses generate jobs, they also destroy large numbers of jobs because of a high failure rate. The economic recession during the 1980s further compromised the viability of small businesses. A sampling of recent articles in the *Wall Street Journal* points to the rise in business failures, especially among small businesses: "Business Failure Rate Grows, Fueling Recession Worries," September 4, 1990; and "Small Companies Lose Big in Retailing War of Attrition," March 20, 1991. A commonly cited statistic is that four out of five start-up businesses will fail within their first five years of operation (Brown, 1988). The failure rate tends to decline for those firms that grow in employment during the critical formative years. Firms that hire one to four people during the first six years face a failure rate of only one-third (Brown, 1988).

Along with the questions about overall employment creation is a growing concern about the types of jobs created. While approximately one-half of jobs created by small businesses are professional, technical or managerial, the rest tend to be low-paying, dead-end jobs. Typically, average wages in small firms lag behind those in large companies. In part, the shift from high-paying manufacturing to lower-paying service sector jobs is to blame for the general decline in wages for American workers. Employment in the small-business sector is also plagued by a lack of health insurance coverate. Approximately 37 million people nationwide, roughly 16 percent of the total U.S. population, lack health insurance coverage. Researchers estimate that about a half to three-quarters of the uninsured population is comprised of small business owners, employees and their dependents (Freedman, 1989; Fritz, 1993).

Asian-owned businesses, particularly those in the ethnic economy, share many of the problems of all small businesses. The brief profile on Asian small businesses in Chapter Four documented why Asian firms tend to be small, have few paid employees, are concentrated in highly competitive sectors, and experience a high failure rate. As stated earlier, employment conditions in Asian-owned firms are not good and ultimately, serve to undermine the minimal standard of well-being for workers and their communities. Average wages in Asian firms are quite low, and work conditions are often substandard. In addition, many owners do not provide health insurance coverage for their workers or themselves. Poor work conditions are further exacerbated by employer-employee relationships, which are often based on ethnic ties. Typically, labor relations are embedded in paternalistic kinship or social bonds, which enable employers to violate standard labor regulations and weaken the potential for worker organizations

(Light and Bonacich, 1988; Ong, 1984). Although ethnic-based work relations provide a degree of cultural continuity and flexibility in the workplace, the broader social costs (i.e., job quality, workers rights, and labor standards) can be quite high. Since most firms involve unpaid family labor, an improvement in working conditions will translate to a higher standard of living for both workers and entrepreneurs alike. Moreover, Asian firms such as garment industry subcontractors are employers of other minorities, namely Latina workers.

Small Businesses and Community Economic Development

Small businesses have historically played an important role in the development of immigrant Asian communities. However, their contribution to Community Economic Development and political empowerment has been limited. Although business ownership is generally regarded as the key to economic success for immigrants, that success comes with high social costs for both immigrants and society at-large. As a result, individual entrepreneurial success is not equivalent to economic development or empowerment as defined by the principles of Community Economic Development. Due to their small size and, more importantly, the socioeconomic costs of small business entrepreneurship, the establishment of more immigrant-owned firms is not a primary strategy for job creation or Community Economic Development.

Although the general characteristics of Asian entrepreneurship clearly demonstrates the marginalized and tenuous position of these businesses, much discussion on economic development continues to center on the further promotion of small business development. The common belief held by policy-makers, officeholders, community representatives, and academics alike is that small business development is the primary strategy for economic development. Substantive discussion on qualitative aspects of economic development, such as the quality of jobs created by small businesses, has been virtually absent from this debate. While recognizing that Asian small businesses play a vital role in economic survival, our emphasis on Community Economic Development does not focus on the promotion of small business development. Our perspective is based on two key reasons: 1) historically, the level of entrepreneurial endeavor in the Asian community has been high due to both structural conditions and access by some immigrants to class and ethnic resources; and 2) the immediate need in our communities requires us to focus on ways to improve the viability of existing businesses and the welfare of ethnic economy workers.

To meet the Community Economic Development objectives of improving the conditions of low-income Asian workers and maintaining the long-term viability of small businesses, the goals of business development must revolve around three basic principles; 1) Asian small businesses should be good employers, 2) Asian small business owners should be socially responsible community members, and 3) business sustainability should be fostered through diversity.

Being a good employer means providing adequate wages, health insurance, a safe and quality work environment, and opportunities for training and advancement. Many of these issues are discussed in detail in Chapter Five. In order for businesses to engage in good employer practices, we recognize that the prevalent conditions of high competition and low profit margins which drive businesses to maximize cost-saving techniques must be addressed. The goal of becoming a good employer is, therefore, intricately linked with the goal of ensuring the long-term financial viability of small businesses, which is discussed later.

The second goal for Asian small business owners is to become responsible members of the community within which they operate. Asian businesses are found in both ethnic enclaves and other minority communities. They provide important services and constitute a critical part of the overall community infrastructure. While social responsibility (defined as societal benefits) is generally considered a requirement of large corporations, it must also be applied to small businesses. No other event raises this concern as clearly as the civil unrest that erupted in Los Angeles at the end of April 1992.

The civil unrest demonstrated quite vividly that Asian small businesses must address concerns of social responsibility, particularly in minority communities. Although the unrest was an outcome of many social ills -- racism, urban poverty, ethnic tensions, and community disinvestment -- it was a signal to entrepreneurs that owning and operating a business does not come without obligations to the community. The point is reinforced by the racial tensions which have erupted between Korean merchants and their African American and Latino neighbors, especially over the proliferation of liquor stores in South Central Los Angeles. Efforts to convert liquor stores into other businesses may serve as a rare example of community intervention strategies, rooted in promoting business social responsibility, that can mitigate some of the negative consequences of free market practices.

Socially responsible practices are becoming a priority for the long-term viability of Asian-owned firms in an increasingly multiracial and multiethnic environment. At a minimum, shopowners must avoid actions which are negligent of their constituencies (Van Auken and Ireland, 1988). Adhering to the principle of social responsibility means that positive customer practices and community relations must be actively cultivated (Joe, 1992). Collaborative efforts such as the Liquor Store Business Conversion Program co-sponsored by a consortium of Asian and African American organizations in Los Angeles are part of an important strategy stressing Community Economic Development.

The final goal of Community Economic Development for Asian businesses is to ensure their long-term profitability by facilitating economic diversification away from narrow entrepreneurial niches. The first two goals of good employer practices and social responsibility are not achievable without meeting this final goal. The uneven concentration of Asian firms in retail trade and services highlights their vulnerability since these sectors are noted for high rates of business failure, vulnerability to economic fluctuations, and extreme competition (Amsun, 1977, p. 84). Consequently, Asian-owned businesses typically have low annual revenues and a high turnover rate, and tend to create low-wage and low-skill jobs.

Conditions of high competition and low profits compromise the work environment for workers in Asian-owned businesses. Employers will typically seek to lower labor costs in order to squeeze some profit out of their businesses either by employing family members at no pay or securing a cheap and vulnerable labor force comprised of co-ethnic or immigrant workers. To address this problem, strategic planning and technical assistance must be provided to help diversify businesses and facilitate their expansion beyond limited geographical boundaries and ethnic niches. Recognizing this situation, a group of Asian entrepreneurs met to discuss possible strategies for diversification (Watanabe and Lim, 1990). In addition to diversification, Asian businesses need to increase the size of their operation, and depart from the abnormally high proportion of sole proprietorships (Amsun, 1977).

Increased international competitiveness has forced U.S. transnational corporations to transverse the globe in search of ever cheaper sources of labor and production methods. Immigrant enterprises, however, have emerged as a valuable source of cheap labor right here at home. Through such linkages as franchising and subcontracting, immigrant businesses provide direct and indirect benefits to corporate capitalism at the expense of both immigrant labor and entrepreneurs (Light and Bonacich, 1988). Research is necessary to examine the feasibility of linking up Asian businesses with growth industries in the local and regional Los Angeles economy such as light manufacturing and transportation to insure long-term viability. Asian involvement in the formulation of regional industrial policy is also critical to creating economic policies that will improve conditions for both entrepreneurs and workers.

Assessment of Current Programs

In this chapter, we assess two types of assistance to small businesses: 1) loan resources for business capitalization, and 2) technical assistance for business formation and various aspects of business operation (e.g., marketing analysis, management, and accounting). Within these two major categories, there is an array of programs offered by a) private nonprofit organizations such as Coalition for Women's Economic Development, Community Development Bank, Asian American Economic Development Enterprises, and the Economic Resources Corporation; b) local and city agencies such as the Community Development Department and Mayor's Office of Small Business Assistance/City Economic Development Office; c) state programs including Small Business Loans Guarantees; and d) the federal Small Business Administration, which provides a variety of loan programs including the Section 8(a) Business Loan Program.

The programs which provide technical assistance are also offered at various levels and are just as numerous: a) private nonprofit/community organizations which include Asian Business Association, Valley Economic Development Center, Pacific Coast Regional Small Business Development Center, and Pacific Asian Consortium on Employment; b) local agencies such as Community Development Department, and Mayor's Office of Small Business Assistance; c) state programs through the Office of Small and Minority Business, and Small Business Advocate; and d) federal programs through the Minority Business Development Agency (Los Angeles MBDC).

Our extensive examination of these various programs resulted in identifying only a few programs significant enough to warrant a substantive assessment. In addition to the governmental programs, we discuss programs offered by local nonprofit community organizations. Our assessment of these programs, both public and private, will be based on how effectively they meet the three goals of creating good employers in Asian business owners, promoting social responsibility, and fostering the diversification of businesses.

Federal Small Business Administration

The Small Business Administration (SBA) is an independent federal agency created by Congress in 1953 to counsel, assist and protect the interests of small businesses in order to preserve the competitive enterprise and strengthen the national economy. The principle activities of the SBA are 1) financing programs, and 2) business development programs which entail individual consultation, conferences and workshops on various aspects of business start-up and operation.

The primary financing capital program offered by the SBA is the 7(a) General Loan Program. The Economic Opportunity Loan Program provides direct funds from the SBA and is specifically targeted to minority entrepreneurs. However, these funds are extremely limited. The SBA prefers to use their funds to guarantee loans which enables them to leverage more from their limited resources. In fact, approximately 90 percent of the agency's total loan effort is represented by the 7(a) General Loan Program, which promotes small business development with loan guarantees of up to 90 percent of the amount provided by commercial lenders (SBA, 1992). In 1991, the SBA provided a total of 1,315 direct and guaranteed loans (excluding disaster loans) to small firms owned by Asian Americans, American Indians and other minorities (excluding African-American and Latino-owned businesses). The loans were worth $425.6 million. In light of these statistics, it appears that the rate of Asian participation in SBA financing programs is quite negligible. Asian-owned businesses number over 300,000 nationwide. Less than one-half a percent (.43%) of these firms participated in the 7(a) General Loan program. Moreover, this statistic is slightly inflated because the SBA lumps American Indian and "other minorities" with Asian-owned firms.

According to two SBA representatives, over the last 20 years, the volume of loans made to Asians in Los Angeles, particularly through conventional lenders and SBA guaranteed loans, has increased dramatically. Approximately one-third of SBA loans through conventional lenders are made to Asian Americans with the bulk made to Koreans (Capgart interview, 1993). This observation was confirmed by the SBA Division Director, Michael Lee, who noted that among Asian ethnic groups, Koreans have been most aggressive in seeking

SBA Loans and have an "intense drive to be independent" (Lee interview, 1993). Part of the reason for this volume of Korean participation is the existence of Korean-owned banks, which provide entrepreneurs access to loans. Lee noted that there is a tremendous need for capital which is only partially met by informal sources. In contrast, other Asian ethnic groups including Chinese and Southeast Asians tend to rely on their own resources and are not major recipients of SBA loans. Although the SBA does conduct community outreach and educational efforts, Lee observed that this task is extremely difficult due to the diversity of ethnic communities in Los Angeles. Lee also noted that a common complaint about the SBA is that it does not solve all problems in small business development. This complaint may, in fact, be due to unrealistic expectations since the SBA often does not have the capacity to address all issues. Another problem is that the SBA does not provide equity capital, which must still be generated by traditional methods such as savings and personal loans. Moreover, requirements in the application process may be prohibitive due to language barriers, bad record keeping, and poor tax paying records of applicants.

Two key SBA technical assistance programs targeted to disadvantaged individuals are the 8(a) program which provides assistance toward certification to participate in government procurement or federal contracts for services and goods; and the 7(j) program which provides managerial/technical assistance, such as consultation on bookkeeping, production, engineering, and other aspects of operating a small business. In 1991, 1,458 8(a) contracts were awarded to firms owned by Asians, American Indians and "other minorities" nationwide. These contracts were worth $1.04 billion. Approximately 979 Asian, American Indian and "other minority" firms participated in the 8(a) program nationwide. This share represents less than one-half a percent (.32%) of all Asian businesses nationwide that are in the 8(a) program. Similar to the statistic for Asian participation in the 7(a) General Loan Program, the Asian share is slightly inflated because the SBA statistic includes American Indians and "other minorities." It is quite apparent that Asians do not receive financial or technical assistance proportionate to their representation among minority small businesses and small businesses in general.

Finally, with respect to community development objectives, SBA focuses its resources on capitalization, minority procurement capacity, and business operation. It provides little leadership or resources for business development concerns beyond those directly related to small business initiation and operation.

State Enterprise Zones

Enterprise zones in the City of Los Angeles are designated by the state as economically depressed areas targeted for economic revitalization and investment. Currently, there are five Los Angeles Enterprise Zones: Central City (East of USC), Greater Watts, Eastside, Pacoima, and San Pedro/Wilmington. Small businesses located in these zones may take advantage of benefits in the form of tax and hiring credits, and local expediting assistance. Because minorities often make up the population of areas targeted by enterprise zones, benefits for communities can come in the form of employment or small business assistance.

Basically, the enterprise zone program provides incentives for businesses to locate in the area as well as hire from the local community. Incentives include a reduction in taxes on employee wages, business equipment expenses, and taxable income. The program is primarily concerned with stimulating business investments and creating jobs in depressed areas. While these objectives seem ideal for areas in need of employment and revitalization, there is no discussion about the "quality" of the jobs created. Since Asian small businesses tend not to generate well-paying jobs for minorities or co-ethnics alike, their location within an enterprise zone would not necessarily improve working conditions for their employees, even with tax and hiring credits.

Moreover, due to the way the program was conceptualized and designed, the issues of human relations and socially responsible business practices are not addressed at all. The concept also is an inadequate response to changes in the economy, insofar as it does not provide industry-specific incentives geared to business conditions in the area. Although enterprise zones may provide an alternative niche for Asian small businesses, the program does not provide any way of determining what that niche will be.

The enterprise zone program has raised concern over what some see as the exploitation of community resources and cheap labor. The zones have been criticized for creating "sweatshop" type jobs (Kennedy, 1986). Massey (1982) has argued that the enterprise zone rhetoric "conceals a completely one-sided shift -- in terms of financial gain and unfettered power from labor to capital."

Finally, the supposedly positive benefits of enterprise zones are yet to be seen. Since the Clinton Administration will place particular emphasis on enterprise zone programs to ameliorate urban decline, the Asian community must make its specific concerns known at both the federal and state levels. At the local level, Asians must also participate by evaluating the local agency's effectiveness. They must offer input on areas needing improvement and suggest changes, so that the program can be more effectively administered. Labor advocates and low-income groups must also offer their critical assessment of enterprise zone programs before wholeheartedly endorsing them.

In attempting to revitalize a disinvested urban area, policy-makers must distinguish between investment and community development. The enterprise zones may translate into investment but not necessarily development. Development is concerned not only with the physical environment but also with the human potential in the community, the empowerment of its members, and the collective benefit, not individual profit, that results from investments (Kennedy, 1986).

Local Programs

The City of Los Angeles Community Development Department (CDD) was founded in 1977 to administer Los Angeles' share of the federal government's Community Development Block Grant (CDBG). In 1984, CDD created the Industrial and Commercial Development (ICD) division to address specifically the economic development needs of low to moderate income neighborhoods. Through the ICD, a portion of the city's CDBG funds are utilized for direct low-interest loans to expand the number of locally owned small businesses. ICD provides assistance in the form of financial lending and entrepreneurial training to businesses that "offer public benefits to low and moderate income residents" through job creation and retention, elimination of slums, and increasing the availability of goods and services. ICD assists a range of established businesses from small "mom and pop" enterprises to major real estate developers. The basic criteria is that projects must provide public benefits which, at minimum, is one new job for low and moderate income residents for every $20,000 in loan proceeds. Priority for loans is given to businesses located in the census tracts where a majority of residents have low to moderate incomes.

ICD offers a variety of programs to help launch new enterprises and assist established businesses achieve financial viability. The programs include a) Small Business Fund (SBF) which provides direct low-interest loans in the amount of $10,000 to $1,000,000; b) bond financing program for large-scale projects of $1,000,000 to $10,000,000; c) Small Business Fund Outreach which provides technical assistance and below market interest rates to businesses in targeted communities;

d) Business Assistance Centers (BACs) in the target communities of Pacoima, South Central and Eastside to help potential entrepreneurs with technical assistance in Marketing/Business Plan, Counseling, and Training; and e) Entrepreneurial Training which provides self-employment training to prospective low-income entrepreneurs and fledgling businesses.

The stipulation of job creation is an important step toward expanding the benefits of small business development beyond the individual entrepreneur. The next step is to ensure that the jobs created are good jobs, i.e., that they provide a living wage, health insurance coverage, and safe working conditions. Aside from adhering to federal law which mandates that CDBG-funded construction projects pay workers "prevailing" wages, the ICD program does not stipulate additional conditions in its discussion on job creation.

Also, the target communities for Business Assistance Centers (BACs) do not currently include low-income Asian communities. The primary objective of BACs, moreover, appears to be the expansion of business development opportunities rather than providing resources and assistance to existing small businesses to achieve the community development goals of becoming good employers, promoting social responsibility and diversifying economically.

As discussed earlier, programs are needed to help Asian-owned businesses move out of limited economic niches. Entrepreneurs need programs that will help them to develop a business structure and plan, find an appropriate site, and improve business management and marketing techniques. However, this type of assistance fails to address the poor working conditions and high social costs of immigrant small businesses. Technical assistance programs such as Entrepreneurial Training can benefit by expanding its mission to deal with Community Economic Development needs by addressing merchant-customer relations, employer-employee relations, and long-term financial viability.

Community-Based Programs

There are many community-based small business assistance efforts. The following discussion covers only a few examples. The Pacific Asian Consortium on Employment (PACE) recently introduced a five-week comprehensive training course for low-income entrepreneurs which covers business start-up and necessary skills such as bookkeeping, financial management, marketing analysis, advertising, and borrowing. This intensive training also addresses finding a niche and how participants can live with little income for the first three years of business operation. Although it is too early to assess the success of the program, the initial evaluation indicates that participants are learning sound business practices. But while this type of technical assistance is important, it nonetheless ignores broader concerns of business development beyond the individual entrepreneur.

Based in San Francisco, Asian Inc. is a nonprofit community-based agency that provides business development assistance to entrepreneurs along with programs dealing with affordable housing development and restoration. Its Business Department provides assistance in the areas of business start-ups, loans for existing small businesses, and government contract procurement. Again, the assistance is focused on business start-ups.

PACE and Asian, Inc. provide valuable resources to entrepreneurs. However, there is still a need for training in the areas of strategic planning, employer responsibility, and customer relations. Since the average Asian-owned firm employs less than four employees and often relies on unpaid family labor, procurement of government contracts means little to most businesses. Programs are needed that address hyper competitive conditions, and that can help diversify and move Asian small businesses into new areas.

The Valley Economic Development Center currently offers the Fledgling Business Program, which is funded by the City of Los Angeles Community Development Department (CDD). The program was recently extended for another year of operation. The program places primary emphasis on job creation through business expansion. Only new and small businesses located in Los Angeles are eligible for the program. The business can be from any industry (such as retail or manufacturing). Participants pay a fee of $198 and make a commitment to hire at least one additional person upon completion of the program. The program consists of class sessions on strategic planning, competitive analysis and advantage, marketing strategy, operations and financial management, and leadership development. The program also provides business counseling and mentoring. After completing the program, a follow-up session with the business is done on a quarterly basis.

In the first year, 200 businesses were enrolled in the program, and 200 jobs were generated, which went mostly to low- and moderate-income persons. The program may have Spanish and Korean language capability by this coming year. Some businesses which have gone through the program have expanded into new markets, or have even merged with other businesses in the program. In most cases, the program has helped businesses expand their operations and profits, which enabled them to hire an additional worker. The results of program have already received high praise from the CDD staff.

Although it is too early to assess the contribution of this program on Asian small businesses, there is no question that it is valuable. Since low profit margins represent one key problem for Asian small businesses, assistance in business expansion may help them diversify beyond the ethnic economy. The program includes training in the traditional area of business management and operation, as well as assistance in strategic planning.

While the program places great emphasis on job generation, it is not clear whether any consideration is given to the "quality" of these jobs. Also, it is not clear whether the program addresses broader Community Economic Development goals such as owner-customer relations and employer-employee relations.

Conclusion: A Community-Based Approach

Our evaluation of existing programs shows that these programs fail to provide extensive resources to assist Asian small businesses meet Community Economic Development objectives. Technical assistance programs typically center on business operation, management, and marketing analysis. These programs currently do not include educational and training opportunities to help facilitate the expansion of minority businesses into industrial sectors where minority entrepreneurs have historically been excluded, such as skill-intensive services (Bates, 1985, pp. 549-552).

Although there are a few exceptions, most existing programs work from the traditional free market view which sees small business success as dependent on the availability of capital. Therefore, most public and private programs are devoted to increasing the availability of and access to venture or finance capital. While capital is indeed important for business formation and viability, capital resources alone are unable to address the broader problems of business practices. Thus, part of the problem is the need to expand the definition of business development beyond the free market emphasis on individual profit. Programs need to address broader community goals and not simply standards of business competitiveness.

Specific public policies must be developed to improve the viability of existing Asian-owned businesses. Currently, policies are aimed primarily at expanding business opportunities rather than providing strategic development planning that would enhance the economic soundness of small businesses. In most Asian communities where there is already a high rate of entrepreneurship, creating new business opportunities is not a high priority. Improving the long-term sustainability and livelihood of existing businesses will not only ameliorate conditions in low-income and minority communities but also reduce the social and economic costs of immigrant entrepreneurship. Considering that small businesses have a largely untapped potential to improve the health of local economies, public policies must address entrepreneur needs in ways that promote public goals such as creation of quality jobs with better wages (Mokry, 1988).

A community-based approach to business development can result in potential benefits for a disadvantaged community and a struggling entrepreneur alike and result in new economic strength, physical upgrading, improved community life, and quality employment (Joe and Eckels, 1981). Moreover, because small businesses are organized around owner-worker and merchant-customer relationships, improving the viability of small businesses could transform small businesses into institutions that can help Asian immigrants integrate into urban society and contribute meaningfully to the local economy.

Policy Recommendations and Strategies

To help meet the three goals of creating good employers, fostering social responsibility, and promoting economic diversification, we propose the following recommendations to community representatives, organizations and policy-makers.

1. Since the nature of small business formation (i.e., reliance on low capital, ethnic networks, cheap labor) limits the size and profitability of firms, organizations must provide knowledge, assistance, and resources to facilitate their diversification and expansion.

2. Community organizations should assist in the formation of a health insurance purchasing group. The Council of Smaller Enterprises (COSE) in Cleveland, Ohio, may serve as a possible model. COSE, the small business division of the Chamber of Commerce in Cleveland, Greater Cleveland Growth Association,

formed an independent health insurance purchasing group, COSE Group Services, Inc. in 1983.

3. Community organizations should develop programs which can do outreach and education to Asian small businesses, particularly those operating in minority communities to encourage and facilitate social responsibility and improved neighborhood relations; these organizations should provide bicultural education for merchants and neighbors, strive to improve customer relations, encourage the hiring of local residents, and promote involvement in local community affairs.

4. Policy-makers need to better link immigrant enterprises to the greater Los Angeles/U.S. economy; they need to help identify economic growth areas and provide strategic planning for development.

5. Small businesses should improve access to health insurance through health insurance purchasing alliances and lobby for small business tax credits, and support a national health care policy that would ensure health coverage for all.

CHAPTER SEVEN

Affordable Housing: Objectives and Strategies

Housing is a fundamental need, essential to individual and community well-being. While employment training and business development policies take precedence by increasing earning power, affordable housing is crucial to establishing a basic quality of life, allowing residents the peace of mind and energy to focus on school, work, and social relationships. The unfortunate reality is a growing numbers of Asians in Los Angeles who cannot afford decent housing and who do not benefit from federal, state, or local housing programs. Consequently, our communities need an affordable housing strategy, which together with improved employment opportunities can contribute to building economically and socially vibrant communities.

Constructing, rehabilitating, and maintaining affordable housing are important components of Community Economic Development. First, providing affordable housing to low-income members of the community is a much needed direct service. Second, quality housing improves the neighborhood itself, resulting in a better living environment for all residents. Third, a better environment can attract private investments in housing and businesses that may not have been available before. Fourth, involvement in housing development and maintenance can strengthen Community Development Corporations through the influx of resources and the capacity to provide more comprehensive services.

We start with the premise that both renters and homeowners have the right to decent, affordable housing. The goal for Asian American communities is to increase the availability of housing for all its residents. Carrying out this goal involves the following objectives:

- Increase affordable housing stock
- Improve and preserve existing affordable housing stock
- Increase rental and mortgage subsidies/financing

The strategies to meet these objectives are:

- Require long-term affordability
- Increase tenant involvement
- Encourage mixed-income neighborhoods and housing

While each objective and strategy contributes to achieving the overall goal, a viable Community Economic Development approach must strive to accomplish all. This chapter begins by describing the decline in affordable housing during the past two decades. Next, we discuss policies and programs that meet the three objectives listed above, as well as Asian American participation in these programs. The last sections address strategies and the role of nonprofit developers.

Affordable Housing Crisis

Even 20 years ago when substantial federal support for subsidized housing existed, the loss of low-income housing units outpaced new housing construction. Instead of primarily benefiting low-income households, federal policies provided greater financial rewards to private developers through tax-shelter benefits. Not surprisingly, private developers have sold, converted or abandoned their low-income projects since the late 1980s as tax benefits were depleted or eliminated. The dearth of quality low-income rental units constitutes a significant problem in ethnic enclaves that face increasing demand due to immigration, and loss of units due to deterioration, demolition and conversion.

The housing gap widens every year. The National Coalition for the Homeless (NCH) found that while one inexpensive unit existed for each low-income renter household in 1970, a gap of 4.2 million units had developed by 1990 (NCH, 1992). The gap may even be greater because many affordable units are actually occupied by residents who are not poor. In Los Angeles City, an estimated 58 percent of renter households cannot afford HUD's "fair market rents" of $684 for a two-bedroom apartment (NCH, 1992), and the problem will become worse because the number of families is increasing twice as fast as the supply of housing (HPPD, 1991, pp. 11-13).

This housing crisis has affect many low-income Asians. In Los Angeles County's low-income Asian neighborhoods, approximately 80 percent of Asian households making less than $20,000 pay more than 30 percent of their income towards rent. Approximately two-thirds of Asian Americans are renters in the three low-income communities described in Chapter Two. Because many Asian Americans earn low wages, only 36 percent of those between the ages of 25 and 64 working at least half-time earn enough to afford the fair market rent (PUMS, 1990). This means that many residents cannot pay for decent housing unless the household has two or more wage earners. With most of their income going toward shelter, low-income Asians have limited funds for food, medical care, transportation and other essentials. The large proportion of income going towards rent also reduces savings that can go toward education or other needs.

To respond to the housing crisis, we need to examine viable alternatives. The next section focuses on programs and policies that attempt to increase the stock of affordable rental units.

Federal Policies to Increase Affordable Housing

Public policy on affordable housing has shifted over time from the construction of government-owned housing projects to privately-owned but government-subsidized housing. As one of the first federal programs to house low-income households, government-owned public housing continues to shelter millions nationwide, but most of the existing 1.3 million public housing units were built before 1970. With very little new construction in recent years, new low-income families can move in only when others move out. In the City of Los Angeles, fewer than 50 public housing vacancies open each month, while over 20,000 applicants wait hopefully for public housing (Housing Authority, 1993, p. 4). Faced with the impossibility of meeting the need for public housing, the Housing Authority even closed the waiting list in June 1992.

In the 1970s and 1980s, government relied on private developers to build affordable housing through the use of tax incentives. But the 1986 Tax Reform Act eliminated most of the tax incentives to build or rehabilitate rental housing and created in their place, the low-income housing tax credit. The tax credit marks the first time that a substantial tax incentive has targeted only low-income units. California added a companion state credit program, both administered by the California Tax Credit Allocations Committee (CTCAC).

Tax credit is a potentially important means of financing nonprofit low-income housing development. Nonprofits can sell the tax credits to banks, corporations, or private investors. The sold tax credits will then be used for equity investment in housing development. The for-profit partner gets a return on its investment in the form of a reduction in its tax liability, approximately 70 percent of the cost of building or substantially rehabilitating low-income units. The developer uses the credits over a period of ten years.

By its legislative mandate, tax credit programs stimulate affordable housing construction and rehabilitation. Tax credits account for 94 percent of affordable rental units being produced nationwide, approximately 120,000 units each year (Cohen, 1992). Since its inception, the federal tax credit program has contributed to the development of over 420,000 rental units (U. S. Senate, 1993). Authorization for the tax credit program expired on June 30, 1992, but housing advocates expect the Clinton Administration to extend this program.

Unfortunately, tax credit programs are insufficient to meet the extensive need for affordable housing. In 1989, demand for the credit was 142 percent of the total credit available nationwide (Racaniello, 1991). In 1991, the Allocation Committee in California received 181 applications requesting a total of $92.7 million federal credits but only had enough credits to fund 78 projects (CTCAC, 1992, p. 2). Moreover, rising costs have cut into the production of units. The average credit allocated per unit for California was $7,141 in 1990 and increased to $9,647 in 1991 (CTCAC, 1992, p. 2).

The severe lack of affordable housing finally spurred Congress to pass the National Affordable Housing Act of 1990 to revitalize efforts to meet low-income housing needs. For the first time since Congress passed its first housing act in 1937, the 1990 Act decentralized federal housing programs to the state and local level. This allowed state and local governments to further tailor programs to meet the specific needs of each jurisdiction. The major element of the 1990 Act is the HOME Investment Partnership Program that provides grants to states and localities to operate rental and home ownership programs.

The 1990 Act included several ways for nonprofit community organizations to become actively involved in the production and operation of low-income housing. The growing role of nonprofits was driven by Congressional concern that earlier reliance on for-profit developers had resulted in short-term, rather than long-term, low-income housing.

Acknowledging the role of nonprofits, Congress mandated that at least 15 percent of HOME funds go to community-based nonprofit housing groups. A jurisdiction can use some of these set-aside funds for technical assistance, training of nonprofit housing groups, or upfront costs incurred in planning a project. In order to receive HOME funds, states and localities must prepare a Comprehensive Housing

Affordability Strategy (CHAS) that outlines the jurisdiction's housing needs and plans. Citizens, nonprofit community housing developers and other interested parties have an opportunity to influence state and local governments because the 1990 Act requires community input in developing the CHAS. The CHAS may also allow community members to monitor the use of federal funds to meet the needs and goals outlined in CHAS.

Local Policies to Increase Affordable Housing

In recognition of the importance of affordable housing, the City of Los Angeles created the Housing Production and Preservations Department (HPPD) to manage the myriad of housing programs. The HPPD's program provides funding for pre-development (appraisals, feasibility analysis, environmental studies, etc.), acquisition and/or "gap" assistance (the gap being the difference between a project's actual development costs and the amount of debt that the project can support). Projects that best fit into the character of a community and that provide benefits such as childcare or social services for the neighborhood receive priority in the selection process.

Local housing departments are not the only ones to provide affordable housing; redevelopment agencies are also mandated to add to the stock of affordable housing. However, the contribution of community redevelopment programs has been relatively minor despite the immense power of these agencies.

California shifted the focus of its redevelopment policy from urban renewal to expanding the supply of low- and moderate-income housing in 1971. Recognition of the importance of affordable housing, especially in redevelopment areas, is codified in the requirement that a minimum of 30 percent of all new and rehabilitated housing units developed in a project area by the agency, and 15 percent by other entities, be low- or moderate-income housing. An agency that destroys or removes low- or moderate-income housing units during redevelopment in a project area must build or restore an equal number of replacement units within four years. In addition, the state adopted a new law in 1976 requiring redevelopment agencies to set aside 20 percent of their agency's tax increment for a low- and moderate-income housing fund (L&M Fund).

Despite the mandate for low-income housing, redevelopment agencies have not significantly addressed housing needs. Fifteen years after the L&M Fund was created, redevelopment agencies are still inconsistent in their calculation of the 20 percent set-aside. Some agencies interpret the requirement to be based on "gross" increments before paying off affected taxing agencies (i.e., other public entities that would have received the increment in lieu of the redevelopment agency), while others use "net" increment after sharing the increments with affected taxing agencies in pass-through agreements. Even legislators are unsure of the correct formula. In state hearings where this inconsistency was discovered, senate members "thought," not knew, that the proper calculation should be based on the gross increment, which generates more revenue for L&M Funds (Senate Committee on Local Government, 1991, p. 3). The lack of clarity in statutory interpretation and enforcement demonstrates the low priority given to affordable housing.

What money that does go into the L&M Fund is often unused. In 1989-1990, revenues from California's 364 redevelopment agencies totalled $3.6 billion (Senate Committee on Local Government, 1991, p. B-5). Funds in L&M accounts totalled more than $450 million, but only $280 million was available for immediate use (Senate Committee on Local Government, 1991, p. B-6). The Los Angeles Community Redevelopment Agency spent almost $69 million of its L&M Fund in fiscal year 1989-90, but still left almost one-third, $26 million, of the fund unused (Department of Housing and Community Development (HCD), 1991, Exh. C). Even worse, the Long Beach Redevelopment Agency spent $1.2 million and left available $2.6 million.

The lack of use of L&M funds prompted the California legislature to pass the so-called "Use-It-Or-Lose-It" statute in 1988. The statute requires redevelopment agencies to spend their excess L&M Fund or give it up. An agency with more than $500,000 in its fund or with a five-year accumulation of set-asides has an "excess surplus." Agencies that do not spend this surplus within six months of the end of the fiscal year must develop a five-year expenditure plan or give the funds to a local nonprofit or housing authority within five years from the date that the surplus was declared.

The dismal record involving L&M funds has occurred despite the flexibility permitted in the use of such funds. By law, redevelopment agencies may use the low- and moderate-income housing funds to increase, improve, and preserve the project area's supply of housing. However, not all funds have to be spent on physical construction or repair. Permissible uses include subsidies to persons and households of low or moderate incomes, as well as for principal and interest payments on bonds and loans, and planning and administrative costs directly related to affordable housing. Often redevelopment agencies have shied away from new construction or rehabilitation and spent the L&M Fund on housing subsidies.

The records of the Los Angeles Community Redevelopment Agency (CRA) show its preference for subsidies rather than construction or rehabilitation. The CRA provided subsidies to 1,260 low to moderate-income households, but built and rehabilitated only 235 units in 1989-90 (HCD, 1991, Exh. I). In total, the agency reported a net gain of 3,331 housing units between 1987 and 1990 (Senate Committee on Local Government, 1991, p. B-10). Although the agency provided a few families with affordable units, redevelopment as a whole did not have a significant impact on the overall needs of low-income families.

Preserving Affordable Housing

Another approach to affordable housing is rehabilitation. Improving the quality of existing housing enhances the living conditions of residents. About 40 percent of all housing units in Los Angeles are 40 years or older, and the percentage is higher in many low-income neighborhoods. Rehabilitating existing buildings to meet health and safety standards transforms them into decent liveable units and an asset that improves the character of the entire neighborhood.

HPPD has five programs that deal with preserving and rehabilitating the existing stock of affordable housing: Neighborhood Preservation Program, Contract Rehabilitation Program, Neighborhood Housing Services, Homeowners Encouragement Loan Program, and the Handyworker. The first three programs are available only for properties located in project areas. Project area boundaries are chosen according to census tracts in which 51 percent of the residents have either low or moderate incomes. Within these project areas, field offices or community organizations operate the specific programs.

The Neighborhood Preservation Program gives out loans and provides technical assistance to rehabilitate single and multi-family residences. The loans are provided at rates below market rate. They are used to help property owners rehabilitate their structures to meet building codes and energy conservation standards. Tenants can be assisted through rent subsidies and/or special financial terms with the property owners, which allow the rents to be kept affordable. The areas serviced by this program are: Pacoima, Northeast (Highland Park/Cypress Park), Echo Park, Boyle Heights/El Sereno, Hollywood,

West Adams, Watts, Chesterfield/Crenshaw, and San Pedro/Wilmington/Harbor (CHAS, 1993, p. 75).

The Contract Rehabilitation Program finances community organizations to actively pursue rehabilitation in their areas. The organizations are responsible for community outreach, program marketing, technical assistance for owners seeking loans, loan disbursements, and monitoring the rehabilitation that takes place. Currently there are only four areas that are selected: Vermont/Slauson, Slauson/Avalon, Florence/Avalon, and Kendren Park (CHAS, 1993, p. 86).

The Neighborhood Housing Services Program focuses on rehabilitating housing and addressing social and economic issues for community revitalization. It operates within four specific areas: Boyle Heights, Crenshaw, Vernon/Central, and Barton Hill/San Pedro (CHAS, 1993, p. 91). Its function is to bring together residents, business leaders, and local government representatives. The goals are to improve housing and living conditions, encourage self-reliance, plan improvements in city services, and encourage community involvement and development.

The Homeowners Encourage Loan Program operates citywide to provide loans to low- and very low-income homeowners to correct building code violations. The Handyworker program is operated by community organizations and is available to owners of single family homes that have a household income less than 80 percent of the Los Angeles County median. The program provides material grants of up to $2,000 for minor home repair.

HPPD also handles HOME funds that can be used for rehabilitation of single family properties. The funds can be in the form of interest-bearing loans, non-interest-bearing loans, interest subsidies, deferred payment loans, or grants (ICF, 1992, p. 3-7). The funds are used by homeowners who have incomes that are less than 80 percent of the county's median income.

Rental Subsidies and Mortgage Assistance

Housing subsidies can provide quality, affordable housing to these low-income residents, both as renters and homeowners. The federally supported Section 8 program for renters give preferences to the homeless and households that pay over 50 percent of their income for rent. Section 8 has two components, vouchers and certificates. The voucher subsidy pays the tenant the difference between the fair market rent and 30 percent of the tenant's household income. However, the tenant qualifying for the subsidy must locate a unit that meets HUD's housing quality standards for decent, safe and sanitary housing. Many program recipients need assistance simply to find such apartments.

The certificate program uses the same qualifications as the voucher program but instead of giving the tenant a subsidy, the public housing authority enters into a contract with the tenant and the owner of a building. If the building meets HUD's housing quality standards, the owner then receives the difference between what the tenant can pay (30 percent of income) and the fair market rent for the type of housing in the area.

The certificate program also requires that housing units be rented to low-income and very low-income families. Low-income families are defined as those whose incomes do not exceed 80 percent of the median income in the area (U.S. Congress, 1991, p. 105). Very low-income families are defined as those whose incomes do not exceed 50 percent of the median area income. In selecting families to be assisted, preference will be given to those that occupy substandard housing at the time of application. Qualified families include those who are homeless or living in shelters. The program also gives preference to families that are involuntarily displaced or are paying more than 50 percent of their income for rent.

Low-income residents also receive assistance that helps them become homeowner. In 1977, the federal government passed the Community Reinvestment Act (CRA). CRA requires all federally chartered institutions to serve the communities they are located in. Serving those needs means providing low-income areas with loan programs for housing, small business, and community development. CRA was designed to eliminate the practice by financial institutions of redlining low-income and minority areas, which accelerated neighborhood decay due to the lack of loans for revitalization efforts. Loans from financial institutions are needed to help sustain a community by providing affordable mortgages and supporting residential improvement and rehabilitation. The Bank of America, after its merger with Security Pacific, set the CRA goal of providing $1.2 billion annually for home loans, low-income housing development funding, and long-term financing of low-income housing (Hirunpidok, 1992). CRA does open up opportunities for low-income areas but there needs to be stronger enforcement of CRA regulations so that financial institutions will better serve communities.

The HOME program offers funds for first-time homebuyers who are low income (incomes less than 80 percent of the median income).

The funds can be used for acquisition, acquisition and rehabilitation, or new construction of homes (ICF, 1992, p. 4-1). For acquisition, the funds can be used to help pay the downpayment of a house through a grant or deferred payment loan. The HOME funds can also be used to pay all or some of the closing costs. Funds can also be used for "gap" financing, which makes up the difference between the purchase price of the home and the sales price that the low-income purchaser can afford. HOME funds can lower the monthly mortgage payments through a prepaid interest subsidy in which the funds are granted to the lender (ICF, 1992, p. 4-13).

An Emerging Crisis

A major weakness of federal policy is its reliance on the private-sector, which has resulted in the pre-payment and expiring use restrictions crisis. Under some federal housing programs established in the 1960s, government-subsidized, privately-owned housing projects have low-income use restrictions. Unfortunately, the restrictions are limited to a certain time period, usually the life of the mortgage, after which the private owners may convert to high cost rentals or condominiums, or even demolish the buildings. Often, HUD offered owners an option to prepay mortgages without HUD approval after 20 years, freeing the owners from use restrictions. Thus, in addition to subsidies and tax shelters, private owners can end up with a very profitable housing project when the use restrictions expire.

The proportion of affordable housing units affected by expiring use restrictions is staggering. In 1987, the U.S. Conference of Mayors predicted that 200,000 to 900,000 units could be affected by 1995. Los Angeles has 11,000 units facing this problem (Sengupta, 1993). Responding to the displacement of low-income tenants, Congress included in the 1990 National Affordable Housing Act a provision that prevents owners from prepaying without HUD approval. In exchange, owners have the option of obtaining additional financial incentives or selling to new owners who qualified for incentives and agreed to maintain affordability restrictions. Recipients of the additional incentives must preserve affordability for the remaining useful life of the project or for no less than 50 years. This effectiveness of this effort depends on funding for the incentives. HUD estimates incentives will cost $2.9 billion in fiscal year 1993, and the cost will rise in the future (Lazere et al., 1991, p. 56).

Future funding is problematic given recent trends and the current budget problems. Funding for HUD's subsidized housing programs fell more than 81 percent from a peak of $32.2 billion in fiscal year 1978 to $11.7 billion in 1991 after adjusting for inflation (Lazere et al., 1991, p. 30). Meanwhile, housing subsidies that primarily benefit middle- and upper-income families have grown significantly. In fiscal year 1990, total direct spending on federal low-income housing assistance was $18.3 billion (Lazere et al., 1991, p. xvii). Yet the federal government subsidized four times that amount, or $78.4 billion, through mortgage interest and property tax deductions, benefiting middle- and upper-income families. With 81 percent of the tax benefits on deductible home mortgages going to the top 20 percent of households, most of these deductions benefit high-income households (Lazere et al., 1991, p. xvii). About 90 percent of the tax benefits from deductibility of state and local property taxes were expected to go to the top 20 percent of households in 1991 (Lazere et al., 1991, p. 36).

Asian American Participation

With the exception of senior citizens, few Asian Americans receive housing assistance. For example, public housing projects contain few Asian American residents. Latinos and African Americans make up the largest groups of public housing residents at 66 and 27 percent respectively. Asian Americans constitute the next group with 1,545 residents, or about 5 percent (Housing Authority, 1993, p. 13). One reason for this low percentage may be the lack of projects near Asian American communities. The exception is William Mead, located near Chinatown, which has 22 percent Asian American tenants.

Similarly, Asian Americans appear to be underserved by low-income housing constructed with tax credits. A telephone survey of the 1990 credit recipients in Los Angeles County showed that less than 6 percent of the units built with credits housed Asian Americans. One reason for the low rate of participation may be because only a few Asian American for-profit and nonprofit developers take advantage of the program (currently there are one for-profit group and two nonprofit groups). Also, because many low-income Asian Americans live in ethnic enclaves, they are unlikely to have access to such units in other parts of the city.

Asian participation is hard to measure at HPPD because projects are awarded through an RFP process, and there are few Asian American nonprofit developers. HPPD does not do community outreach. The RFP (Request for Proposals) is the key process for nonprofits to learn about and apply for project funding. HPPD deals mainly with nonprofit groups that have been in the community for a long period of time and have demonstrated the ability to build affordable housing.

Currently, 20 nonprofit groups participate in HPPD's programs. While these groups cover almost every part of the city, there is no Asian nonprofit development corporation included. One reason may be the limited number of Asian nonprofit housing developers. However, the Korean Youth and Community Center (KYCC) has received funding from HPPD to build a 19-unit apartment building that will include office space for KYCC. There are also plans by HPPD for seven affordable housing projects (382 units) within the Westlake area that contains large numbers of Filipino Americans and Korean Americans (Doherty, 1993).

The poor performance by redevelopment agencies limits their role in alleviating the housing crisis in Asian American communities. However, active citizen direction of redevelopment efforts may change this situation. Chinatown is the only one of the three case study low-income communities in this book located within a redevelopment project area. Since its inception in 1980, the Chinatown project area has gained 860 new and 260 rehabilitated units. However, information on the number of housing units destroyed is unavailable. City officials are considering redevelopment projects for both Koreatown and the Asian American neighborhood in Long Beach. Given the mixed reviews on redevelopment, we are uncertain as to the benefits of these projects.

In terms of rehabilitation and preservation, a few of HPPD's programs operate within low-income Asian American tracts in our three case study communities. However, there are no program areas that contain a particularly high concentration of Asian Americans. The HPPD programs described above could be used by Asian Americans if the programs were targeted to our communities. The three low-income areas in our study contain single-family and multi-family units that could use rehabilitation. With the availability of 1990 Census data, Asian American advocacy groups should actively identify census tracts that meet program guidelines.

Relatively few Asian Americans receive rental subsidies. The Housing Authority does try to outreach to all ethnic groups and publishes pamphlets in ten languages, but few Asian Americans use the Section 8 subsidy programs (Clark, 1993). In 1991, a little over one percent, or 910 persons, of those who used the Section 8 program, were Asian Americans (Housing Authority of City of LA, Statistical and

Demographic Overview, 1991, p. 13). The largest minority group that uses the program is African Americans at 69 percent, or 48,232 persons. The disparity in usage is particularly sharp considering the nearly comparable size of the Asian American and African American populations in Los Angeles County.

The Role of Nonprofit Developers

By definition, a Community Development Corporation (CDC) serves low- and very low-income tenants, and is committed to long-term housing affordability rather than short-term profit. In a National Congress for Community Economic Development survey conducted in 1991, an estimated 2,000 CDCs across the country had built close to 320,000 units of affordable housing (NCCED, 1991, p. 4). In California, nonprofit development projects constituted 42 percent of the award recipients in 1991, which is far greater than the legislated minimum of a 10 percent set-aside for nonprofit projects (CTCAC, 1992, p. 7).

CDCs are usually based in poor communities that have minimal public and private investments. CDCs take a comprehensive approach to housing, targeting special populations, as well as provide supportive services tailored to meet the needs of residents. For example, Asian American CDCs can provide additional services to tenants, such as translation help, counseling, and job training. Moreover, as part of its broad approach to housing, CDCs usually encourage local control and have built-in mechanisms for tenant involvement in the operation of the housing project.

Community development corporations compete with as well as surpass for-profit developers in providing affordable housing to low-income individuals and families. What CDCs lack in experience and resources, they more than compensate for in their mission to build, rehabilitate, and operate decent, affordable housing for their community without the expectation of a high rate of return.

Development costs for affordable housing match those of market-rate units. According to a new study jointly sponsored by the Local Initiatives Support Corporation and the California Tax Credit Allocation Committee, no systematic difference in development costs exists between market-rate housing and affordable housing projects (1993). However, the study pointed to many restrictions that can increase costs in an affordable housing project. For example, these projects have twice as many financing sources as market-rate projects. The juggling of these funds increases the complexity and duration of the development process. Streamlining the process will improve the efficiency of affordable housing production.

Nonprofit developers and community development corporations already are taking the lead in providing affordable housing. As discussed earlier, nearly one-half of the projects receiving tax credit awards were those of nonprofit groups. The ability of CDCs to successfully compete for tax credits reflects a match between their mission and the public goal of affordable housing.

Although Los Angeles is home to many established and new low-income Asian American communities, few nonprofit housing developers or CDCs target Asian American communities. There have been some community-based efforts to build affordable housing such as senior housing -- Cathay Manor in Chinatown and Little Tokyo Towers -- but these efforts are not ongoing. The development efforts are usually one-shot projects. Currently, the Little Tokyo Service Center is the only ongoing CDC that has built affordable housing. As we will discuss in Chapter Eight, nonprofit Asian American social service agencies and business associations abound. But the trend for participation in low-income housing development is just starting.

Due to their general lack of experience in housing development, Asian American nonprofit developers need technical assistance (Kim, 1993). KYCC, for example, has contracted with consulting firms to help build their affordable housing project. While the sharing of knowledge among Asian American communities is already well established in the social service arena, it has barely started in housing development. The guidance of ongoing CDCs will allow others to build up experience, expertise, and familiarity with funding sources.

Tenant Rights Among Asian Americans

Because increasing the supply of affordable housing is a slow process, the immediate problems of most renters must be addressed through tenant rights. Problems for low-income Asian American tenants are similar to those of others: increasing rents, unexplained charges, illegal and unsafe conditions, and wrongful evictions. The problems for Asian immigrants are compounded two-fold. First, many low-income tenants do not complain about housing conditions due to unfamiliarity with their rights as well as fear of eviction. Second, organizations providing assistance and legal services to tenants are extremely limited in the Asian American community.

Few government housing programs require tenant participation, and examples of tenant organizations are usually the result of unusual circumstances. The occasional emergence of tenant organizations, tenant/management corporations, and tenant-initiated lawsuits to improve living conditions has been in response to crises rather than for empowerment. For example, the prepayment problem caused tenants to organize to fight prepayment or form cooperatives to buy the housing project from the owner. Thus far in Los Angeles, only one group of tenants, the Mission Plaza Tenants Association, has signed a purchase agreement and is applying for HUD financing to buy their apartment building (Sengupta, 1993). Thus, even with a crisis as a stimulant, tenant empowerment is rare and often limited in scope.

More often, individual tenants seek to redress housing problems through the legal system. While organizations like the Legal Aid Foundation provide services to low-income individuals and families, the Foundation does not have the capability to assist monolingual or limited English speaking Asian Americans. Asian American clients represent approximately 2 percent of Legal Aid cases (Interview with Nakamura, 1992). In 1991, Legal Aid sought to remedy this problem by working with the bilingual staff at the Asian Pacific American Legal Center.

Conclusion: The Need for Housing Strategies for Asian Americans

The above evaluation of needs and existing programs shows that there is a lack of any coherent low-income housing policy for Asian Americans. Few Asian American tenants are benefiting from current housing policies and programs. Yet, there is a significant number of Asian Americans who cannot afford decent housing. The government should recognize this need and try to adapt policy to meet it.

Government involvement is not itself a solution to the needs of Asian Americans. Asian Americans ourselves must get involved in the process. We should advocate for housing programs to be inclusive of the Asian population and become proactive in developing affordable housing. Long-established community service centers need to consider the possibility of developing decent, affordable housing for the community residents who use their services.

In this book, we recommend that nonprofit Asian American community-based organizations help fill the housing void by developing housing. Nonprofit groups have several advantages over profit-driven developers:

- They can provide direct housing assistance
- They are committed to long-term, low-income housing development (rather than short-term profit motive)
- They are interested in a comprehensive approach to housing: a mixture of services supporting the various needs of residents
- They permit greater local control and individual empowerment
- They produce social benefits besides housing

In order for Asian organizations to build affordable housing, they must work with other Asian or non-Asian nonprofit developers to gain experience in the field. They should attend workshops with other neighborhood nonprofit groups to educate themselves about nonprofit development, and coordinate their efforts to avoid competition with others for scarce government subsidies and resources.

Policy Recommendations and Strategies

1. Direct public capital grants to finance an increasing share of production and acquisition of housing.

2. Develop standards of adequacy that realistically reflect cost of housing and non-shelter necessities.

3. Make housing an entitlement benefit for low-income households.

4. Develop appropriate housing schemes for large households (disproportionate growth of affordability problems among large households; broaden definition of family to include traditional and non-traditional arrangements). Housing design with supportive social and community services, as well as economic policies (Stone, 1990, p. 49).

While affordable housing is the main theme in this chapter, the whole community should not be comprised entirely of low-income units. Mixed-income units and neighborhoods promote an integrated class community and erase the stigma associated with low-income housing. This will allow for integration and interaction among different income classes, which will be beneficial to the community. The mixture of housing units may also increase the cash flow of the project, so that it can receive larger loans to build additional low-income units.

With quality, affordable housing as well as market-rate units within the community, residents increase their options. Many residents within low-income communities often move out when they pull enough resources together. They move to gain access to quality housing, larger units, or lower home prices outside their community. In mixed housing communities, residents have more options. A community should meet the needs of all residents, and it should be a place where all are proud to live.

PART III

IMPLEMENTATION THROUGH INSTITUTION BUILDING

CHAPTER EIGHT

Internal Organizational Capacity

Key to successful Community Economic Development is a community's ability to control its own development. Middle and upper class communities often have the resources to secure the changes they want for their neighborhoods. Low-income communities usually do not. In Chapter Nine, we will show why public and private institutions oriented toward community development often have negligible Asian involvement and, in turn, underserve low-income Asian populations. There is a critical need to develop institutions rooted in low-income Asian communities so that residents can direct development. These institutions must be able to carry out the key CED functions: 1) to deliver services to help people overcome economic obstacles, 2) to conduct direct "community-building" work, and 3) to plan and direct the community's overall development. In all these activities, institutions must be accountable to and insure the participation of residents.

This chapter evaluates the capacity of institutions within Asian communities to undertake Community Economic Development. A viable foundation requires three elements. First, there must be institutions that can carry out the various aspects of CED. Second, there must be adequate financial resources to sustain these institutions. Third, there must be an adequate supply of people with the necessary skills and training. Our analysis shows that considerably more work is needed in all three areas. Further, as CED is undertaken by organizations, there must be institutionalized means through which accountability to the community and involvement of residents are insured.

Institutions in Asian Communities

While there are some pan-Asian organizations, most institutions in Asian American communities are built along ethnic lines -- i.e.,

Chinese, Korean, Vietnamese, etc. These latter institutions arise from the extremely diverse histories, cultures and languages of the various Asian groups. To carry out CED activities, organizations will initially need to be similarly ethnically oriented. Since most low-income Asians are recent immigrants with limited English skills, providing services in native ethnic languages becomes a practical necessity. Further, the sense of a common ethnic identify, particularly among recent immigrants, is an important foundation for effective organization.

This single ethnic-orientation, however, creates difficulties given the ethnic diversity of most geographic areas with a high concentration of Asian Americans. As documented in Chapter Two, Asian populations tend to concentrate in specific geographic areas, such as in Koreatown, but these neighborhoods are also contains a significant numbers of other ethnic and racial groups. Ethnically-based organizations operating in geographic communities must address this complexity through linkages with other ethnic organizations (see Chapter Nine).

What is the existing institutional capacity in Asian American communities to carry out CED work among low-income populations? While numerous Asian organizations exist, relatively few institutions are oriented towards low-income populations and based in the communities. Most are geared towards the interests of the business and professional classes in Asian American communities. Generally, each Asian American community has at least one chamber of commerce or business association. Some of these groups are loosely organized networks, while others are fully staffed, well-funded and quite sophisticated. There are also networks of professionals, such as the ethnic bar associations. In addition, broader advocacy or civil rights organizations such as the Japanese American Citizens League (JACL) and Chinese American Citizens Alliance, have historically drawn active members from the ranks of businesspersons and professionals.

Business and professional classes in Asian American communities are able to build a strong institutional "infrastructure" because they have greater resources at their disposal. They raise funds among themselves, and have access to other funding sources. By virtue of their professions, they typically have greater organizational skills and time flexibility. Because of all the same factors, low-income people, particularly recent immigrants, face many obstacles in building institutions that can serve their needs.

Asian communities are also rich in religious organizations. Churches are probably the largest community institution with a base among low-income Asians. They serve crucial spiritual, social and cultural needs, but historically have not been active in economic or political activities. Moreover, their primary mission can bias a CED strategy because they tend to exclude non-church members. While it is beneficial for community organizations to work with church groups, we do not see church-related groups as the primary vehicle for CED.

The other main community institution oriented toward low-income Asian populations is the health and human service sector. Generally, social service agencies are fairly developed. Many have relatively long histories and established reputations, offer a sophisticated range of programs, and operate with substantial funding from public and private sources. Because of their community orientation, reinforced by funding requirements, most of their services are geared toward low-income people.

Among such agencies, Community Economic Development is a relatively new endeavor. There are few organizations that are dedicated to CED work. There are, however, a number of institutions that carry out specific aspects of CED work geared towards low-income Asian communities -- advocacy, services, physical development and community development planning.

Many of the advocacy organizations are not CBOs, although few focus on the economic concerns of low-income people. The groups with a broad agenda include the Japanese American Citizens League, Asian Pacific Americans for a New L.A., the National Coalition for Redress and Reparations, Korean American Coalition, and the Asian Pacific American Legal Center. The human service sector does advocacy work that affects low-income Asians because they are their service population. Individual agencies take up limited advocacy work, usually around specific programs and policies affecting them. In Los Angeles County, many agencies coordinate such efforts through the Asian Pacific Planning Council (APPCON), a coalition of health and human service agencies (Ching, 1993).

The area of CED work most commonly addressed by Asian organizations is job training. Within APPCON, these agencies include Chinatown Service Center, Korean Youth and Community Center, United Cambodian Community, and Pacific Asian Consortium in Employment. However, other needs such as workers' rights education and tenant rights advocacy receive less attention.

Business development work is a relatively new activity for Asian American organizations. Typically, this aspect of CED is carried out by Community Development Corporations, or CDCs. CDCs carry out direct "community-building" through 1) business development including financing, investment and assistance, and 2) physical, "bricks and mortar" development of industrial and commercial facilities, affordable housing and community facilities. Asian community organizations that provide business development assistance include the Pacific Asian Consortium in Employment (PACE), United Cambodian Community, and Asian American Economic Development Enterprises (AAEDE). There are only a handful of organizations that are building low-income housing or community facilities. Little Tokyo Service Center is the only ongoing Asian American CDC that has actually completed a housing project. KYCC is also in the process of building low-income housing along with a community center. Meanwhile, other organizations have expressed interest in getting into community development.

A final area of CED activity is community development planning. Institutions are needed to strategically plan and direct the overall development of the community in a way that strengthens its economic health and improves the quality of life of residents. Such direction includes economic development planning, which in large part takes place through linkages with governmental agencies in charge of such policies (see Chapter Nine). In addition, community planning also includes overseeing the building and maintenance of infrastructure (roads, sewers, energy), the impact of transportation (public transit routes and stations), land use planning (zoning and ordinances), and public facilities (schools, parks, health facilities).

Governmental planning bodies in many poor and minority communities are usually devoid of participation from low-income people. CDCs and other community groups have often attempted to fill this gap and take up the task of community development planning. The problem is that such efforts require certain kinds of expertise and a lot of resources, particularly if one is serious about actually involving low-income residents in the planning process. Currently no Asian community organization engages in this type of planning work as an ongoing function.

Community Groups and Financial Resources

CED is geared towards low-income communities, but these communities cannot generate the funds needed to carry out this work. External resources must be found to sustain CED institutions. Most community organizations do independent fundraising including soliciting individual contributions, and holding fundraising dinners. Unfortunately, such efforts generate only a fraction of the funds organizations need. Most organizations must therefore rely on a combination of government and private foundation monies.

Most funding sources provide funds for specific programs rather than for general operations. Because organizational survival is at stake, it is very easy for community-based groups to become "funding-driven" -- to shape their agenda to activities for which funding is available. This creates the potential for tension between what the community needs and wants, and what programs private foundations and government agencies are willing to fund. For instance, there are state and federal funds for job training and business development training and assistance. For other aspects of CED, such as workers' and tenants' services, advocacy work, community organizing, and community-based planning, there are few available funding sources (Ching, 1993). Not surprisingly, these CED activities are rarely found in community organizations. For instance, advocacy must usually be done on top of the work and time funded for service delivery, usually by overburdened executive directors.

Since the demand for services usually outstrips the capacity of agencies, "extra" time for advocacy work is extremely limited. This is also the case for coalitions like APPCON. Since APPCON itself receives little operating funds; much of its advocacy work must be carried out by the same agency executive directors. In addition, many agencies feel constrained by their relationship with government departments, who often become the target for advocacy work, but are also the funding sources for the agency's programs (Ching, 1993).

Funds for housing and community development have been drastically cutback at the federal level (see Chapter Seven), but there still exist various sources of funds that can be used for "community-building." Funds are frequently restricted to the design and construction of the project, leaving little for staff and organizational operating costs (Sugino, 1993). "Developer fees" from completed projects or from rent from commercial property can be a source of funds for operational expenses. The problem is that such funds all follow from the successful completion of projects. Asian CDCs, therefore, face tremendous difficulties getting off the ground. Further, developer fees are often not enough to fully sustain the operation of CDCs, even with successful projects. The lack of funds creates a "chicken and egg" barrier for Asian community organizations. Without initial funds, there can be no CED activity, but without CED activity, there can be no regular source of income.

A further problem is that most governmental and private development financing sources exclusively target housing. There is very little for construction of community centers, youth facilities, childcare centers, recreational or cultural facilities, etc., which are all just as vital to improving the quality of life for residents. Such projects generally rely heavily on private fundraising and contributions. Needless to say, low-income Asian communities themselves are unlikely to generate the monies needed.

Unlike development financing, funding for job training and other social services is, by its nature, primarily to pay staff to carry out these activities. This, in itself, helps to sustain the organization in a way that development financing does not. Service funding contracts include amounts for administration of these programs, which helps to insure that such programs contribute to sustaining the organization because they pay for administrative and management staff as well as operating costs. Still, organizations are left with little flexibility to do much else beyond specific programs that receive funding.

A final problem is that government and private foundation support has often excluded Asians. The needs of low-income Asian communities rarely figure prominently in the economic development plans and programs on federal, state or local government levels. For example, the Los Angeles Community Redevelopment Agency recently initiated a new program to give selected nonprofit housing developers $150,000 over three years for operating expenses. The recipients included a Skid Row housing developer, an organization developing AIDS housing, nonprofit developers based in the African American and Latino communities, but no Asian American organizations despite the relatively large number of Asian applicants.

Since government funding is usually for specific projects, community organizations often turn to private foundations for operating expenses. While some foundations, such as the Irvine Foundation locally, have a record of sensitivity to Asian community needs, most private funders do not. A study conducted of private foundation grantmaking nationally concluded that between 1983 and 1990, less than one-fifth of one percent (.18 percent) of foundation dollars went to Asian American organizations. Of this, about 22 percent went to employment or housing services or activities (AAPIP, 1992, pp. 7-8). In another example, in the first round of "capacity-building" grants to CDCs by the private foundation-funded Collaborative Training for Community Development, Asian communities were excluded -- only CDCs in South Central and East Los Angeles were eligible. No doubt these funding patterns have to do with the widespread perception that Asian communities have few economic problems.

As more Asian organizations move into Community Economic Development work, they will face the additional problem of competing against each other for limited funding. Because Asian organizations doing CED work will likely be ethnic-specific, there could be nearly as many organizations as there are Asian ethnicities (the 1990 Census identifies 19 separate Asian ethnicities). Government agencies and private foundation are only now beginning to include Asian organizations in community development funding programs. Even if Asian community clout with these funders increases and there is greater recognition of low-income Asian needs, there will always be only a few organizations (or more often, just one) that can expect to be selected for funding. It will be critical that strong relationships be built among Asian organizations doing CED work to avoid destructive competition.

To extricate themselves from government or private foundation funding reliance, some community organizations generate revenues through for-profit ventures, such as rent from commercial property. The County's Economic Development Corporation, for instance, relies on rent from an industrial park it owns. The Asian American Economic Development Enterprises, Inc. also relies on rent from commercial real estate. In other cases, organizations generate income through business ventures.

The for-profit option is usually taken up by CDCs that are already in the business of real estate development or economic development work. Needless to say, while the prospect of being financially independent is certainly attractive, these efforts are fraught with risks. Such ventures require large amounts of capital, which is difficult for nonprofit organizations to raise. Also, like any business venture, there is no guarantee of success. Particularly during economic downturns, organizations may find it difficult to find commercial tenants who can pay required rents. Still, as more Asian American community organizations get involved with community economic development, some may turn to commercial efforts for revenues.

Human Resources: The Need for CED Training

Since CED functions are so varied, the expertise needed to carry them out is diverse. Community-based organizations must find the people with the necessary training. This is not easy. Community organizations have not been swamped by large numbers of CED job-seekers. For many, the inherent job insecurity of relying on public or private funding sources (usually temporary) is unattractive. Pay and benefit levels are generally below comparable private sector jobs and often even below civil service employment. As a result, most community-based organizations tend to take on younger people recently out of college, often without the skills specific to the job. In some instances, organizations are staffed by local residents or previous "clients" of services the organization provides.

The higher education system generally does not meet the training needs for CED work in Asian American communities. Few departments on college campuses have links with community organizations. Asian American Studies programs are an exception. These academic programs make students aware of community organizations and career opportunities with them. Unfortunately, there has been relatively little research, even in Asian American Studies, to the economic concerns facing low-income Asian populations. This tends to limit the number of students attracted to Community Economic Development, or to organizations carrying out such work.

A few university departments offer coursework and training for carrying out CED work. Staff in the social service organizations today tend to have backgrounds in social welfare, public administration and social sciences. These fields are consistent with the predominant social service orientation. The skill and training needs for CED work, however, are different from those provided by these departments. CED requires a practical understanding of economics, government policy and programs, training in business and planning skills, as well as a social and political understanding of Asian American communities and their relationship with other communities. Business schools, public policy and administration programs, and law schools all offer students some courses related to particular aspects of CED work.

Urban planning programs offer the most comprehensive training experience suited to CED work. In particular, UCLA's Urban Planning program has the potential to provide the policy framework and practical skills for CED work. While it is possible for a highly motivated student to pull together a plan of study that will provide relevant training, the bottom line is that there is no single university program that can provide comprehensive training for undertaking CED work in low-income Asian American communities. In fact, there are considerable barriers to acquiring the needed skills.

As a result of these shortcomings in university training, new hires usually come to community organizations with little background for their job. Moreover, there is not a large pool of experienced job applicants. Because CED work is a relatively new activity in Asian communities, there are not many Asians available with training and experience in economic advocacy, physical development work, or community planning. The organization must therefore bear much of the burden of training. Training must be "on the job," and skill development usually comes through experience.

Training and expertise is particularly a problem in carrying out physical development work and some aspects of planning, because these activities are incredibly complicated and technical. Such work involves a variety of skills, including real estate knowledge, familiarity with design and architecture, experience in dealing with local city bureaucracies and permit processes, and understanding complex government financing programs. There is usually little government funding available for such training. These costs must therefore be assumed by the CDC (Sugino, 1993).

There are some low-cost and free sources of development training that a few Asian CDCs have used. The California Community Economic Development Association (CCEDA), in conjunction with the Los Angeles City Community Development Department, held a collaborative training program on Community Economic Development that included funding for projects. Other nonprofit institutions such as the Legal Aid Foundation, the Center for Nonprofit Management, and the Center for Community Change offer workshops occasionally.

One weakness of such training is that it tends to be adhoc and piecemeal -- it is not easy for a fledgling community organization to acquire a comprehensive set of skills to do CED work. The only ongoing local program that provides relatively comprehensive training is the Los Angeles Collaborative Training for Community Development, which is funded by private foundations such as ARCO, Irvine, Hewlett and others. The Collaborative provides four weeks of intensive training over the course of one year, oriented toward CDCs working on actual projects. The program also offers operating support grants and low-cost pre-development loans to participants. But because participants are selected through a highly competitive application process, only a handful of Asian American organizations can expect to go through this program.

Community Accountability: The Need to Involve Residents

Our vision of Community Economic Development is one where improving economic conditions is not simply done for or to low-income people, but by them. They must gain greater control over economic resources and thereby, their lives, in order for change to be qualitative and sustained. In order for this to happen, there must be institutions through which low-income people can get organized, articulate their needs, and translate their concerns into action.

Vehicles for the participation and involvement of low-income people are very undeveloped in Asian communities. There are few avenues through which poor and working-class people can organize and empower themselves. In CED work, meaningful participation should, at a minimum, include participation in setting priorities and community planning.

Unfortunately, decision-making over development has generally excluded residents. For instance, a number of low-income Asian communities are affected by redevelopment. Chinatown and Little Tokyo are in City of Los Angeles redevelopment project areas. The Hollywood project also includes areas of significant low-income Asian populations. Koreatown is under study by the CRA to become a new project area. The Cambodian community in Long Beach is part of a projected project. Redevelopment project areas are required by law to establish Project Area Committees (PACs) to insure community involvement. But while experiences vary, these PACs tend to have major limitations. First, they are structurally weak in that they are generally only advisory. Actual planning functions rest with the redevelopment agency staff, and decision-making power with the redevelopment agency board and the City Council.

Second, the PACs tend to lack representation from residents, low-income people and their advocates. The members of the Little Tokyo Community Development Advisory Committee (the Little Tokyo Redevelopment project area PAC) include 36 percent local businesspersons, 14 percent representatives of major Japan-based corporations or banks, 20 percent developers or other businesses, only 10 percent representatives from churches or the community groups, and the remaining 20 percent miscellaneous individuals (LTCDAC roster, 1991). This body includes no low-income residents. The local community service organization and CDC, Little Tokyo Service Center, has only this year been added to the body.

The Chinatown PAC had originally been constituted by at-large elections in the community. But when community activists attempted to elect a more grass-roots and less business-dominated slate, the local Councilperson (Gilbert Lindsay) unilaterally dissolved the PAC, renamed it the Chinatown Community Advisory Committee (CCAC) and mandated that all members be appointed. Nevertheless, community members of CCAC feel that despite these weaknesses, CCAC has been able to have some positive influence on the CRA's priorities -- including the building of senior citizen housing and the expansion of Alpine Recreation Center (Toy, 1993). Despite some positive outcomes, it is still clear that the involvement of low-income residents in redevelopment planning processes is generally lacking.

Because of these weaknesses in governmental bodies, it often falls upon community-based organizations to organize and insure the involvement of residents. Methods can vary. For example, seats on the organizational Board of Directors can be set aside for residents, memberships can be extended to local residents, and community meetings can be organized to plan specific campaigns or projects. Participation of residents in strategic planning of the community's economic development is crucial. As discussed previously, the problems facing low-income people is rooted in the economic and physical conditions of the area in which they live. Resident involvement in community development planning should include identifying and prioritizing CED needs, planning for services, directing the overall economic development of the community, identifying specific development projects to support or initiate, and planning an advocacy and broader linkage strategy.

CBOs face numerous obstacles in attempting to build participation. First and foremost is the resource problem. Because of their situation, working people often find it difficult to go to many meetings. Working and raising a family leaves little leftover time and energy. In order for involvement to be meaningful, there is a need for training and education of residents. It is not enough to simply bring residents to a community planning meeting. An effort must be made to familiarize them with the planning process, the way development generally takes place, the possibilities and constraints for development, and the political and institutional players involved. Institutions that want to generate meaningful participation must be able to work with residents over time to lay the foundation for such participation. On top of this, organizing meetings, printing flyers, and putting on activities all take time and money.

Given the constraints on people's lives, it is not realistic to expect that such involvement can be on a volunteer-driven basis. Funds to pay for staffing and organizers are necessary. It is not realistic to expect such funds to be generated from low-income residents -- funds must come from outside the community. There are, however, few funding sources that provide support for organizing work.

There are also structural problems in trying to organize and involve local residents. Many human service agencies have fairly extensive and deep ties with their local communities. Their insights and experiences with these populations can be invaluable in organizing efforts; however, their client-social worker relationship with low-income people, based on the general social welfare approach, makes it difficult to carry out general organizing. As a result, while the agencies provide crucial support services and serve as general advocates for low-income people, they are not well-suited to organize and involve them (Ching interview, 1993).

In other communities, CDCs often attempt to do organizing among low-income residents in the neighborhoods in which they work. Some CDCs have been created through mass movements that spontaneously emerged around a particular economic development issue. People in these mass movements created CDCs as an institutionalized way to maintain community control over economic issues in their neighborhoods. Once such organizations begin to take on development work, it is very easy for them to become subsumed by such work, and for organizing to fall by the wayside. In some instances, organizations that started off with a broad vision of social change for their community have evolved into exclusively project-oriented groups. Over time, organizations increasingly find their "hands tied" as they get into development work. Like human service agencies which feel constrained in targeting their government funders for advocacy efforts, CDCs often feel constrained from confronting banks, real estate developers, and government officials who they must now work with in order to advance their projects (CCC, 1985, pp. 21-25).

These are a few of the challenges faced by community institutions attempting to involve low-income residents. Many well-intentioned organizations have stumbled attempting to overcome these hurdles. At the same time, there are positive examples. Korean Immigrant Workers Advocates, as mentioned before, is one of a few organizations that attempts such organizing work locally. Their goal is to build a membership made up of workers, and they recently decided that workers will have majority representation on their Board of Directors. The Chinatown Resource Center in San Francisco carries out ongoing tenant organizing activities and strives to involve low-income residents in their community planning work. While the hurdles are difficult and resources scarce, the starting point for institutions in low-income Asian communities must ultimately be the recognition of community accountability and involvement, and a commitment to these challenges.

Conclusion: The Need to Create CED Institutions

Much needs to be done to build and strengthen institutions and organizations for CED. Existing service agencies, with countless dedicated staff and volunteers, serving low-income communities, can be a strong foundation. Except for employment training services, Community Economic Development work is relatively new to Asian communities. There is a clear need for aggressive institution-building to strengthen our communities' ability to take on CED work. Whether this means expanding the existing human service organizations or building new institutions will depend on the particular conditions of a community.

Where are the gaps? There is a need for institutions to step up advocacy work around economic issues facing low-income Asian communities; for services geared toward workers' rights and housing problems; for the building of community development corporations with the capability to carry out physical development work, including community facilities and affordable housing; for institutions to carry out community development planning for low-income communities. In particular, there is a need for institutions taking up CED work to creatively meet the challenges of organizing and involving low-income Asians in all of this work.

The issues of funding and human resources for such work are intertwined with building such institutions in Asian communities. Greater funding, training and skills development for the various aspects of CED are needed to help initiate and sustain this work. On the other hand, unless Asian activists and leaders build institutions to carry out this work, funding is unlikely to be found. Further, to avoid competition between communities for scarce resources, strong working relationships between Asian community organizations engaged in CED must be built. Ultimately, the institutions doing CED work will develop to the extent that the economic concerns of low-income Asians will gain greater visibility.

Policy Recommendations and Strategies for Community Organizations:

1. CDCs should be created to do community-building work in low-income Asian communities, and should integrate advocacy, planning and physical development work.

2. Asian American academics must place more emphasis on research and policy work on the economic needs of low-income Asians.

3. People in Asian communities must make a more concerted effort to gain recognition of the economic needs of low-income Asians among policy-makers and funders.

4. Asian community organizations taking up CED work should build working relationships, partnerships and coordination to avoid destructive competition for limited funding sources.

Chapter Nine

External Political Linkages

A viable Community Economic Development strategy cannot focus solely on individual neighborhoods. We must look outside low-income communities for additional resources to carry out the development work and organizing needed to make a significant impact. In addition, external economic and political forces profoundly affect low-income communities; thus, a CED strategy must recognize the need for broad social change, especially in public policy.

Low-income Asian communities must develop linkages with local government agencies, elected officials and private foundations. Influencing these institutions depends on organizing and empowering disenfranchised residents and forming organizations which can advocate for their needs, along the lines discussed in the previous chapter. This chapter discusses the next step, the process of building strategic linkages beyond the neighborhood. This includes electoral work and developing ties with government agencies involved in economic development. It also involves coalitions and alliances with other ethnic communities to develop collective power. However, building inter-ethnic alliances is more than just a strategy for political empowerment. It is a responsibility Asians have living in a diverse and multicultural society.

The final section of this chapter discusses the political content of these linkages. We present a range of policy issues that cannot be addressed at the community level alone and that require government intervention. These issues also provide a foundation for building coalitions with other ethnic communities. Developing linkages is an important part of any CED strategy. As discussed in the first part of this book, corporate policy and global economic restructuring have drastically transformed the local economy, severely limiting economic opportunities in Los Angeles. The flight of heavy manufacturing facilities (automobile, durable goods) to the Third World has meant the loss of hundreds of thousands of high-quality and high-paying jobs. They have been replaced by jobs in the garment, light manufacturing and service industries, where wages are low, working conditions are poor and the mostly immigrant workers are not unionized. Within this low-wage sector, Asian immigrants compete for jobs with Latinos, with African Americans often locked out all together.

Compounding these problems is the flight of local capital from the inner city, leaving a vacuum in retail and commercial services and jobs for area residents. Much of this vacuum has been filled by immigrant entrepreneurs, including many Koreans and other Asians. However, Latino and African American residents, frustrated by limited economic opportunities and government neglect, often see the presence of these small businesses as symbols of their inability to control development within their community. This, along with cultural and language barriers, has led to the explosive race relations facing this city.

This is the sobering context confronting CED efforts in Asian communities. However, by incorporating external political linkages in CED work, residents can change economic conditions, shift the priorities of local government and unite diverse communities. They can also shape city-wide economic development policy and participate in the "rebuilding" of Los Angeles.

Building Linkages to Formal Political Institutions

Political empowerment requires a range of strategies, including the traditional approach of electoral politics. However, these strategies should include non-electoral efforts if they are to be effective. Such efforts are particularly relevant for low-income Asian communities since they are comprised primarily of immigrant populations with limited electoral participation and few resources.

One political empowerment strategy that has attracted much attention is the effort to increase the number of Asian elected officials. Asians are underrepresented at all levels of government, even though they comprise 11 percent of Los Angeles County's population. When more than 2,000 Korean-owned businesses were damaged or destroyed during the civil unrest of April 1992, merchants received little assistance from government agencies. Many Asian Americans attributed this lack of government response to the small numbers of Asian elected officials.

Redistricting is one way to increase the possibility for Asians to get elected, but more importantly, it can improve the impact that Asian voters can have on local elections. In Los Angeles, recent redistricting efforts were led by the Coalition of Asian Pacific Americans for Fair

Reapportionment (CAPAFR), consisting of community organizations, legislative staff persons, academics, nonprofit agencies and civil rights advocates. Members of the coalition testified at redistricting hearings at all levels of government and lobbied extensively to maintain the integrity of Asian communities throughout the county. Its greatest success was in the west San Gabriel Valley, where the Asian population was previously divided into three state assembly districts. The new redistricting plan combines the cities of Monterey Park, Alhambra, San Gabriel and Rosemead into one state assembly district where Asians made up 28 percent of the population, the highest proportion in the state (Kwoh, 1993).

However, efforts to keep the Koreatown/Filipinotown (Westlake) communities in one city council district were not successful. Likewise, even where the integrity of some Asian communities was maintained, the resulting districts still did not have a majority of Asian voters. This was not due to weaknesses in the strategy of the CAPAFR, but because of the dispersal of the Asian population throughout the county. The results of SALIC also show the effects of this dispersal (see Table 1).

TABLE 1: Ethnic Composition by Community:

	Asian	Latino	Black	White
Chinatown/Echo Park	33%	53%	5%	9%
Koreatown/Westlake	32%	46%	7%	13%
Long Beach	19%	34%	20%	26%

Source: SALIC, 1993

Given the demographic realities, efforts to gain political power cannot rely solely on electoral strategies. Asians must also build coalitions and alliances with the other ethnic and minority communities. Despite losing to Richard Riordan, Mike Woo's 1993 mayoral campaign was highly successful in appealing to other ethnic communities on the issues of police reform, economic development, crime and civil rights. His endorsements outside the Asian community included the Mexican American Political Association (MAPA), County Supervisor Gloria Molina and prominent African American leaders such as Councilman Mark Ridley-Thomas.

Asians must also work to increase their influence within political parties. Some communities have party organizations, such as the Pilipino American Los Angeles Democrats (PALAD). These organizations register voters, hold candidate forums, conduct voter education and attempt to project Asian perspectives into their party's agendas. However, most of this work is only conducted during elections, rather than an on going basis. Political action committees (PACS) should be developed as yet another vehicle to impact electoral politics, but because of limited resources, they are not of significant relevance to low income Asians.

In addition, Asian communities must focus on reforming the electoral process itself. In some public school districts across the country, parents of students in those schools are allowed to vote in school board elections, whether or not they are citizens. Similar efforts are needed in Los Angeles so that low income Asians and other immigrants can have a greater voice in local governance. Additionally, more attention needs to be placed on improving the process of gaining U.S. citizenship, since this is the first step toward electoral participation.

However, the election of Asian officials does not guarantee accountability. Many members of the Japanese American community were dismayed when former U.S. Senator S. I. Hayakawa actually spoke out against reparations for those who were interned during World War II. Nor does getting Asian faces into office guarantee results, particularly at a time when government must deal with massive budget cuts. In the last 20 years African Americans have been largely successful in winning the mayorships of major cities across the country. But this phenomena has coincided with corporate disinvestment, capital flight, reduced federal aid and jobs leaving the inner cities. As a result, mayors face greater needs for "social programs within the constraints of the cities' diminishing resource base" (Clavel and Wiewel, 1991, p. 5) and have been severely limited in their ability to improve conditions for their inner-city constituencies.

Thus, Asian support should be given to those who display genuine concern for the community's issues, regardless of the candidate's ethnicity. For low-income Asians, these issues include poverty, low wage employment and substandard housing. But it should be understood that getting individual candidates elected cannot in itself bring about social change, or even just better responsiveness from government.

Nor should empowerment be seen as possible only through the electoral process. Non-electoral strategies can be almost as significant. These strategies include developing ties with the staff persons of elected officials, local government agencies and private foundations. They include advocating for more Asian staff members in strategic and decision-making position. These linkages can ensure that Asian community organizations receive Requests for Proposals (RFPs) and Notifications of Fund Available (NOFAs) from government agencies, gain adequate attention for program needs and be kept abreast of policy and procedural issues.

In Los Angeles' complex network of economic development players, key government agencies are the City's Community Redevelopment Agency (CRA), Community Development Department (CDD), Housing Preservation and Production Department (HPPD) and Housing Authority and the County's Community Development Commission (CDC) and Economic Development Corporation. The mayor has his own economic development staff as well. Local offices of federal departments include the federal Economic Development Administration (a division of the Department of Commerce) and the Department of Housing and Urban Development (HUD). Finally, another key player is the recently formed Metropolitan Transit Authority (MTA). Besides handling the operations and development of the region's bus and rail systems, the MTA will have a significant impact on affordable housing development, job creation and training and other development-related activities. Building a relationship with MTA staff should be a high priority for Asian communities.

Private foundations and organizations should receive equal attention. Many foundations already support CED work, although only a few Asian organizations benefit from this support. A key player in Los Angeles' non-profit development community is the Local Initiative Support Corporation (LISC), which has limited involvement with Asian communities. Some foundations, such as the Irvine and Liberty Hill Foundations, are fairly sensitive to the needs of Asians, but in general most foundations need to be better educated about community needs. Of course, it is not the sole responsibility of the Asian community to educate these foundations and government agencies. These institutions need to take it upon themselves to do outreach and serve a broader constituency.

Economic Development Policy

Within the Asian community in Los Angeles, too little attention has been given to advocacy on economic issues of concern to low income Asians. Some organizations which make advocacy a conscious part of their efforts include Asian Pacific Americans for a New LA (APANLA), National Coalition for Redress and Reparations (NCRR), Japanese American Citizens League (JACL), Korean American Coalition (KAC) and the Asian Pacific American Legal Center (APALC). However, because of the community-wide nature of the issues they address, these and other organizations do not focus on the specific economic needs of low income people. Historically, advocacy-oriented groups have taken up broad issues such as civil rights and racial discrimination, anti-Asian hate crimes, the glass ceiling, immigration and other issues that cut across class lines.

Some human service agencies that serve low-income clients attempt to do advocacy around specific programs and policies, but most agencies acknowledge that the need for advocacy work far outstrips what they are able to do (Ching, 1993). A positive development is the creation of the first national Asian Pacific American Public Policy Institute by the UCLA Asian American Studies Center and Leadership Education for Asian Pacifics (LEAP). One challenge facing this institute will be to take on research on issues vital to the lives of low-income Asians.

Of course, influencing economic policy is difficult for all minority communities, particularly in the absence of any comprehensive or coherent economic development strategy. One recent strategy was initiated in response to the civil unrest in the Spring of 1992, when then Mayor Tom Bradley, with the encouragement of Governor Pete Wilson, established Rebuild LA (RLA), a private, nonprofit organization charged with coordinating comprehensive economic revitalization efforts for the city and the region. A governing board of over 80 persons was appointed to oversee the work of the organization. Besides setting the creation of 60,000 jobs as its primary objective, RLA encourages corporate investment into riot-impacted neighborhoods through an aggressive recruitment campaign, streamlining permit procedures and better coordinating the work of various city agencies.

Regardless of one's analysis of RLA's strategy, which has since shifted to small business assistance, it will continue to play a prominent role in the formation of economic development policy in Los Angeles. However, it is difficult for low-income Asian communities to have a significant impact on an institution that is not a public agency and exists outside the electoral arena. RLA is primarily accountable to its board, which includes nine Asian Americans. In the Asian community, the primary group with access to these board members is APANLA, a coalition of various community organizations and individuals which came together shortly after the creation of RLA. The Asian board members of RLA sit on APANLA's steering committee, formalizing a relationship between the two organizations.

Active members of APANLA are primarily political aides, staff of various government agencies, business persons and other professionals. APANLA's "Rebuild LA" agenda has been effective in bringing attention to the legitimate needs Asian merchants who lost their businesses during the civil unrest. However, more efforts are needed to better involve low-income families, workers and other disadvantaged Asians and to take up their issues.

Asians and other communities have a right to a voice in the formation of economic development policy in LA and the region. However, the fragmentation of city and county agencies involved with economic development (CRA, CDD, HPPD, CDC, etc.) and the existence of institutions like RLA severely limit this voice. What low-income Asians would most benefit from is a local government agency or office with the authority to coordinate the overall city's (or county's) economic development. This agency could also act as a mechanism to involve traditionally disenfranchised communities.

Under Harold Washington, the City of Chicago conducted innovative programs that made the economic development process accessible to local communities. Among these was the Neighborhood Development Program (NDP), which was operated by the city's Department of Economic Development. The NDP demonstrated "that development services could be effectively delivered through community-based organizations" (Clavel and Wiewel, 1991, p. 83). The intent of such programs is to create a process that gives disenfranchised communities input on city-wide policy. Thus, these programs differ from neighborhood development councils or similar bodies which simply encourage "NIMBY" (not in my backyard) attitudes.

Building Linkages with Other Communities

As stated earlier, Asian communities by themselves lack the power to have direct impact on electoral politics and economic development policy. They need the support of other communities. However, conflict between the Asian community and other communities of color in LA has become increasingly prevalent, as economic opportunities decline and each community competes for scarce resources. For these reasons, building alliances and coalitions should be a priority for those working for the general empowerment and economic development of Asian communities. Moreover, participation in these alliances is a responsibility Asians have as members of an increasingly diverse and multiethnic society.

Even before the 1992 civil unrest, a variety of groups in LA attempted to deal with ethnic conflict. One such group was the Black/Korean Alliance (BKA), which was incorporated in 1987 with assistance from the Los Angeles County Human Relations Commission. The BKA attempted to deal with tensions between Korean merchants operating in South Central Los Angeles and African American residents. It established three committees: 1) a community education and cultural exchange committee, 2) an economic development committee, and 3) a religious leadership committee. These committees attempted to bring merchants and residents together and create a working dialogue between these communities.

While the alliance was successful in holding charitable events and establishing a scholarship fund, it was ill-equipped to deal with massive problems such as the continued deterioration of neighborhoods and schools in South Central and the lack of jobs and opportunities for its residents. However, while recognizing that the lack of economic opportunities were at the root of much of the conflict, BKA members were never united on a platform to bring economic development to South Central. Instead, the economic development committee focused on creating partnerships and joint ventures between Korean and African American business owners. Due to its limitations, the BKA disbanded on November 17, 1992.

Other attempts to improve race relations in Los Angeles include various conflict resolution efforts, inter-ethnic relations education, cultural exchanges and even such things as a Black/Korean golf tournament. While all of these efforts play a role, we believe that race relations work should focus on economic impacts and actively involve low income people. One characteristic that Asian, Latino and African American communities all have in common is that significant segments of their populations live in poverty, are unemployed or are stuck in low-wage work. This provides a basis for building better relations among communities and uniting them around a common agenda for economic justice and opportunity.

While such work is very difficult, there are some efforts in Los Angeles which can serve as models. One such effort has been led by former City Councilman Mike Woo and various ethnic banks and nonprofit organizations. This group has created a pool of money for loans to minority businesses in the inner city. Another effort is the New Majority Task Force, which has attempted to unite LA's ethnic communities on an economic development platform. Convened by

Asian, Latino and African American community leaders, the organization held a conference in November of 1989 entitled "Economic Development: The New Majority in Los Angeles." A statement from the conference proceedings summarizes the principles unifying the organization:

> At the heart of the "New Majority" concept is the assumption that members of Los Angeles' various ethnic communities share one key commonality: unequal access to resources and low economic opportunities and achievements in our neighborhoods.

The New Majority's recommendations include 1) redefining economic development to include neighborhood revitalization, community involvement and human resource and job development, 2) utilizing linkages as a strategy to spread development and growth throughout the city (such as requiring commercial developers to contribute to an affordable housing fund), and 3) continuing to strengthen and deepen the new majority coalition (Pastor et al, 1990, pp. 1-4). While the work of the New Majority has had limited impact, it provides the contextual foundation for building long-term relationships between Los Angeles' ethnic communities. Its efforts to organize a grassroots economic development summit in early 1994 shows much promise and may help to fill the current void in community-based economic development leadership and advocacy.

The missing element in most coalition work in Los Angeles is a community education and organizing component, especially one which targets and involves low income populations. Coalitions between communities may exist among leaders, professionals and business persons, but they often lack the involvement of more disadvantaged sectors.

In Los Angeles' labor community, an example of positive efforts to empower these sectors is the work of the Korean Immigrant Workers Advocates (KIWA), which is organizing Korean workers, supporting labor struggles among of unions that are predominantly Latino and African American, and taking up issues that affect workers of all races. Similar efforts are needed if effective coalitions are to be formed. However, low-income communities also have few resources to carry out this work. Thus, it is incumbent upon the business and professional sectors of the Asian community to play a larger role in helping the disadvantaged sectors, including providing resources. Even these more advantaged sectors can reap economic benefits when low income groups are better organized and the community as a whole has better jobs and housing.

A Strategic Approach to Community Advocacy

While linkages create better access to elected officials, government agencies and other institutions, they are of little use without solid policy positions. Linkages must be built on long-term principles, rather than on patronage or "inside" connections. Having clear advocacy positions on economic development policy can help facilitate this process.

While community advocacy must strive for public policy to be more inclusive of Asians, it should also promote recognition of what the community can contribute to the overall society. Asians suffer from the "model minority" stereotype and are often excluded by policy-makers, resulting in the neglect of community needs. But Asians also have much to contribute, including a vibrant ethnic economy, strong community institutions and other resources. They must be part of the development of inner cities, since many of their policy issues are shared with other communities. All of these considerations need to be brought to the table. With this approach, Asians are better positioned to have an impact on policy-makers. They can also work with other communities to expand resources for everyone, rather than fighting for a slice of a shrinking economic pie.

With this approach in mind, the remainder of this section provides a policy framework for the CED component areas of employment, small business development, housing and institution/capacity building. Additionally, it discusses broader policies needed to reinvigorate the regional and national economies.

In employment, the barriers facing disadvantaged Asians include a lack of skills and English ability, severely limiting their access to better paying jobs. These are the main reason that so many Asians are locked in poverty. In addition, most working Asians are concentrated in industries without unions. In the past twelve years, state and federal policy has organized labor and workers' struggles. This is especially alarming in light of the proliferation of low wage jobs and unregulated industries in Los Angeles. Finally, the local and national economy currently shows no signs of generating high paying and quality jobs unless there is significant public intervention. Thus, advocacy in employment should call on policy-makers to recognize:

1) the need for more English instruction and job training programs that target and are sensitive to the needs of low income Asians;

2) that government must play a more active role in regulating the work environment, ensuring fair wages and benefits and supporting the right of workers to unionize;

3) that government must play a more active role in economic development policy, with an emphasis on the creation of quality and high wage jobs accessible to low income Asians and other disadvantaged communities.

Federal policies define small businesses as those with fewer than 500 employees and most programs focus on providing capital for business start-ups and expansion. These programs do not recognize the fact that many Asian and other ethnic businesses are very small and usually have fewer than four employees. These "mom & pop" enterprises are only marginally profitable, often rely on family labor and "sweat equity" (long work hours under difficult conditions) and cannot provide good wages or decent benefits. They are often concentrated in the same retail and service industries and compete against each other. Finally, they are sometimes in conflict with the needs of area residents, as illustrated by the high concentration of Asian-owned liquor stores in South Central Los Angeles. These small businesses need policies and programs which:

1) provide technical assistance to improve-long term viability, including diversification and conversion to other types of businesses;

2) provide assistance in creating quality employment and decent wages and benefits, particularly health insurance for their employees;

3) provide assistance in understanding how to do business in highly impoverished and ethnically diverse communities.

Like many low-income communities, disadvantaged Asians face many barriers to finding quality and affordable housing. Overcrowding and high rent are prevalent, with two, or even three, families often sharing one household. Advocacy efforts in housing should focus on:

1) increasing the stock of affordable housing, as well as developing housing which meets the needs of large families;

2) making housing an entitlement and finding more effective ways to ensure its development, such as direct government subsidies rather than tax credits and other market incentives;

3) changing affordability standards to better reflect the real costs of housing and non-shelter requirements, particularly in LA where the cost of real estate and transportation are so high.

To improve the capacity of Asian communities to control and conduct their own development, policy-makers and funders must recognize the scope and depth of need in low income Asian communities and better include this sector in economic development funding, training opportunities, strategy/policy development and institution building opportunities. Specifically, Asians must advocate for:

1) more emphasis on funding for nonprofit CED work, particularly for fledgling Asian CDCs, as well as greater funding for planning, advocacy and organizing efforts in low income communities;

2) a greater role by those in higher education to help provide training and education for community development research, and to target minority students for such programs;

3) the creation of local structures (such as the Project Area Committees used in redevelopment) to allow for community-based planning, with the election, not appointment of those in decision-making positions, and that these structures involve low income residents and receive adequate funding to facilitate community involvement.

Finally, the effectiveness of Community Economic Development hinges on the state of the regional and national economies. When there is growth, low unemployment and prosperity, community-based groups will have a better chance of achieving their goals. Of course, a robust economy in itself does not guarantee the well-being of poor people. "Trickle down" is problematic, and we have seen that, over time, economic growth has had little to offer the poor. However, a robust economy is an absolutely necessary and fundamental condition for the generation of economic and social wealth. While we believe that unrestrained market activities are partly responsible for marginalizing minority communities, this book does not advocate a simple "supply-side" or "interventionist" approach to stimulating economic growth. The market creates conditions for economic growth and vibrancy, but interventionist strategies are just as necessary to ensure that both economic prosperity and social costs are equitably distributed.

Thus, to create an economic climate favorable to CED, we support broader policies designed to reinvigorate the regional and national economies. There are currently several policy areas that can help foster economic growth including; 1) converting defense industries, 2) reforming government regulation, 3) improving U.S. competitiveness in a global economy and 4) encouraging investment in low-income and minority communities.

In the area of defense conversion, we believe that a more coherent policy is needed. In California, there has been an absence of political leadership to deal with the impact of the cuts in federal spending. Other states, such as North Carolina and Texas, have demonstrated that strategic planning, while not completely eliminating the impacts of base closures and contract reductions, have helped lessen their severity.

What is needed for Southern California is a mechanism to anticipate defense spending cuts, assess their regional impact, plan strategies to absorb displaced workers, and convert military facilities. The federal government offers a variety of programs to help local jurisdictions deal with such issues, including grants through the Economic Development Administration (EDA). However, Southern California's political leadership has been slow in taking advantage of such programs. One reason may be the myriad of jurisdictions which make it difficult to coordinate regional strategies. A regional planning mechanism may be the first step in dealing with this dilemma.

Another issue requiring attention is the regulatory role of government. The number of jurisdictions and government agencies with narrow regulatory functions creates excessive burdens on business, particularly smaller firms. It is often necessary for a new business to obtain permits from several city or county agencies, such as fire, building and safety, public works and planning departments as well as special jurisdictions such as the Air Quality Management District (AQMD). Recent steps by the Los Angeles City Council to create a "one-stop" permit process and to coordinate the role of various agencies are positive steps toward reducing this bureaucratic nightmare. Such services already exist in areas designated state "Enterprise Zones" but need to be expanded to all parts of the city and county.

Third, we support efforts to improve the position of the U.S. in the world economy. The last two decades have seen greater mobility in both labor and capital, and the increased integration of the global economy. The continuation of this process appears inevitable and will have significant impacts on local economic development. To ensure that these impacts are positive, an aggressive state role is needed to foster policies which will help local economies.

Such policies include efforts to eliminate unfair trade barriers that prevent U.S. goods from competing in foreign markets. Regional integration, under certain conditions, may be desirable as well. By reducing trade restrictions and eliminating tariffs between Canada, the United States and Mexico, many economists predict the North American Free Trade Agreement (NAFTA) will lead to long-term economic growth for the entire continent. However, such initiatives require the state to ensure that proper environmental and labor standards are practiced throughout the region and that the industries which benefit from this policy are accountable to local communities.

Finally, we support increased investment in impoverished areas to help them become vibrant communities. Many low-income communities are located in inner-cities where capital flight and job losses have devastated the economic base. This process can only be reversed by concerted efforts to encourage both public and private sector investment. Capital reinvestment in low-income communities can be accomplished through regulatory and market-oriented approaches including initiatives such as Redevelopment, the Community Reinvestment Act (CRA), federal "Enterprise Zones" and tax incentives. We realize that, in the past, these initiatives have not always benefitted the most in need. Thus, we call for the creation of mechanisms to ensure that the most disadvantaged sectors of the community are involved in the process and can reap benefits from such investments.

Conclusion: Beyond Strategic Linkages

One of the most important lessons of the Black Power and Civil Rights struggles of the 1960s was that large-scale social change comes from broad, organized and sustained movements, not from linkages between poor communities and elected officials or existing institutions. For Asians, this lesson means that we need to emphasize long-term community organizing and political education. It also means reaching out to and building coalitions with other communities. Building broad movements is not easy because tangible benefits are not always realized in the short-run. However, Community Economic Development is a way to turn advocacy into action. Through CED, we can build the community-based institutions and linkages needed to develop and sustain our movements.

PART IV

CONCLUSION

CHAPTER TEN

Summary and Framework for Action

In addressing the socioeconomic well-being of low-income Asians in Los Angeles, this book reaches several conclusions:

1. There can be no empowerment for Asian Americans without recognition of the large, often voiceless and invisible population of poor Asians with unmet basic needs.

2. Except for refugee communities, joblessness is less extensive of a factor in low-income Asian communities than other communities of color, as there often exists an extensive enclave economy. Thus, the challenge is not to spur new small business development, but to improve the viability of existing businesses and the quality of jobs they generate.

3. Community Economic Development is a strategy that can effectively address the problems facing low-income Asian communities. An Asian CED strategy must look at Employment, Small Business Development, Housing, Capacity Building and Political Linkages.

4. The April 1992 civil unrest clearly demonstrated that Asian Americans can no longer afford to build economic strength through entrepreneurship while ignoring participation in the political process. Asian Americans must become active participants in policy-making to ensure that all groups are treated equally and fairly.

5. Institution building and strengthening linkages with policymakers, government agencies, foundations and

other ethnic communities are integral to enhancing the Asian community's capacity to carry out Community Economic Development.

6. While Asian communities have many economic needs, they also have many economic strengths. If channelled properly, these strengths can contribute to the economic development of impoverished areas. Thus, Asians must be part of any efforts to "rebuild" LA and revitalize inner-city areas.

Our research from this book reveals an Asian American community in critical need of quality jobs, skill and language training, decent and affordable housing, and assistance in small business development and planning. This research dispels the myth that Asian Americans are enterprising and prosperous. A substantial number are members of the working poor or are among the jobless. They face barriers that trap them in ethnic enclaves, where living and working conditions are often very poor.

Caught in the vicious cycle of trying to "make ends meet" for themselves and their families, low-income Asians lack the skills and language ability that could lift them out of this substandard existence. As long as poor Asians make up a substantial segment of the Asian population in Los Angeles and no effort is undertaken to improve their socioeconomic status, any strides made by other Asians are illusory.

Like others in the U.S., low-income Asians are entitled to a better standard of living and a decent quality of life. They have a right to meaningful employment that provides a living wage, opportunity for mobility, stable housing, and other important necessities of life. However, current Asian community organizations are primarily engaged in social service delivery. While their services are vital, they tend to treat only the symptom, not the larger problem. CED offers another perspective -- one that offers empowerment as well as services. Rather than focusing on deficiencies, CED strategies enhance a person or community's level of skills, abilities and resources. They build on these strengths to legitimize rather than marginalize low-income communities. Asian community-based organizations are beginning to recognize this and are moving into community development work.

The task of looking at the needs of Asian Americans and developing a framework for economic development can be directly tied to the effort to rebuild Los Angeles. The rebuilding effort can finally provide the opportunity to address the issue of economic inequality in the Asian American community. Avoiding the issue of inequality and the needs of Asians at the bottom of the ladder, we believe, will cause any rebuilding effort to fail.

In addition to calling for justice and equality for the Asian community, we call for a renewed spirit of social activism. Economic development combined with organizing and advocacy can produce positive changes and give voice to the working poor. It is imperative that community groups, churches, unions and other organizations educate themselves and their members about the economy and how to best shape policies to reap tangible benefits for their communities.

As long as the needs of low-income Asians continue to be ignored by policy-makers, elected officials and community representatives alike, true democracy for Asian Americans is unattainable. Low-income Asians will remain voiceless and invisible. We must ensure that low-income Asians, like all other impoverished communities, have access to economic opportunities. Anything less would be a false democracy.

A Five-Year Action Plan

We recommend that Asian communities take three broad steps to implement the CED goals outlined in this book. They should:

1. Encourage organizational capacity building
2. Promote internal and external linkages
3. Generate innovative projects that have a broad impact on economic development policy

Each step is not meant to be exclusive of the others. In fact, some steps must be done simultaneously. We do, however, suggest that a particular step receive greater emphasis at a specific time. The following description shows how these steps would fit into a five-year timeframe.

Capacity Building (One-to-Three Years)

While there are a few Asian community organizations with experience in Community Economic Development work, most groups lack the organizational capacity to do this work. Therefore, the first priority is to build and strengthen capacity.

First, community-based organizations (CBOs) interested in CED work must obtain operating funds to hire staff for such work. Second, training and technical assistance is needed, particularly for projects involving affordable housing and other developments. To meet these needs, organizations should link up with resources such as the Los Angeles Collaborative for Community Development, which provides training and operating grants for affordable housing development; approach private foundations for operating grants; and attempt to open up new sources of funds and training, such as recent overtures by Asian community representatives to Housing and Urban Development Secretary Henry Cisneros.

Board members, staff and clients of these CBOs must be involved in the development of this work. Capacity building must include a process of educating organizations and their boards about the work they will undertake. It must also include creating ways to involve community residents in planning efforts -- to insure that they are participants in determining the priorities of projects and the goals of CED work.

Capacity building should also include learning from similar efforts in other communities across the country. Connections should be made with Asian groups involved with CED in San Francisco, New York, Boston and other cities. Local organizations with some expertise in CED work should share experiences with fledgling organizations.

Ultimately, this capacity-building step will enable community organizations to successfully launch projects, including affordable housing, community development and planning, and employment training and small business assistance.

Internal and External Linkages (Two-to-Four Years)

As Asian CBOs gain experience in carrying out development projects, the question of building linkages will emerge as the next major step. Internal linkages between Asian communities and CBOs will be necessary to expand CED work. External linkages to political institutions, relevant economic development agencies and other communities will be essential in insuring full inclusion of Asians in broader economic development policies and programs.

As Asian CBOs build their capacities, they can end up competing for the same private or governmental funding. Mechanisms to encourage coordination and cooperation will be critical to avoid a destructive and self-defeating level of competition. The Asian Pacific

Planning Council (APPCON) provides an example of how Asian CBOs can coordinate similar service programs and pursue joint funding. This is particularly crucial since funding sources often use implicit racial criteria in awarding funds. This means that for any given funding, only a few Asian organizations will receive an award. Sharing information about various funding sources and program opportunities, encouraging joint projects and proposals, collectively lobbying, and, where possible, prioritizing needs can help to minimize competition.

External political linkages will also be crucial for Asian communities. Because of the civil unrest of 1992, the current economic recession, down-scaling of the defense industry and general concerns about global restructuring, development policy enjoys a high level of public attention. New program initiatives will emerge from various levels of government, the private sector and foundations. Asian CBOs need to build external linkages to ensure that they are "in the loop" when these initiatives are debated and implemented.

These external linkages include building ties with local political institutions, elected officials and key government and private agencies, as outlined in Chapter Nine. They also include efforts to increase Asian political representation. Asian CBOs must strive to access existing funding sources as well as participate in the development of policy. However, this means Asians must be prepared to contribute to the economic development of the broader community and region. The welfare of low-income Asians is inextricably tied to the welfare of all who are economically marginalized.

Finally, linkages with other communities are important. As discussed in this book, many of the needs of low-income Asians are shared by other low-income minority communities. At the same time, many of the tensions between ethnic communities are rooted in economic conflicts. Building coalitions and ties with African American and Latino organizations, labor unions and other institutions will be important to bring about policies that will benefit all communities.

Innovation and Impact (Four-to-Five Years)

As Asian CBOs build their capacities and linkages, they will be in a position to create innovative programs. This step represents a crossroads for Asian communities. Because many organizations remain dependent on specific government and private sources of funding, it is easy for such organizations to become "funding-driven." That is, the organization's activities are shaped by the requirements of funders rather than an independent determination of needs. This is problematic since our analysis has determined that *many existing policies and programs are ill-suited to the CED needs of low-income Asian communities.*

Asian CBOs in this third stage must develop innovative programs. Organizations will have the track record and stability to experiment and attempt new pilot programs, as well as the experience and insight to understand what is feasible. This can include program concepts mentioned in this book, such as small business diversification and upgrading, worker organizing and education efforts, and specialized employment training for better paying jobs.

By building the linkages described in the previous stage, Asian CBOs should be in a position to influence broad economic policy. Currently, this policy is shaped without the involvement of disadvantaged communities. "Public-private partnerships" in economic development typically involve only governmental agencies and business representatives. Asian CBOs, together with groups from other minority communities, must push for inclusion in this process. Policies must be rooted in daily grass-roots struggles and shaped by a new inclusionary vision.

To accomplish this third step, it will be necessary for Asian CBOs to reexamine their experience, broadly evaluate existing programs, and synthesize any critiques. There must be a forum that can bring together key actors for an extended dialogue. The objective is to identify major gaps in CED activities and target a few priority proposals. These can serve as a platform for a concrete campaign to change the way government and foundations address CED in Asian communities.

Conclusion

These three steps provide a strategic plan for CED work in Los Angeles' low-income Asian communities. The plan should not be interpreted rigidly, since each community and its institutions face different conditions. The value of this plan is that it can serve as the basis for keeping CED work accountable to constituents, as well as promoting innovative approaches to the problems facing disadvantaged communities.

APPENDIX

Survey of Asians in Low-Income Communities (SALIC)

The purpose of this survey is to gather information that would supplement the Census data. Although the 1990 Census provides an extensive amount of demographic and economic statistics, information on Asian Americans is often reported for geographic units that are larger than what we consider to be a neighborhood. Moreover, the Census does not collect data on the employment history of workers, the ethnic characteristics of their workplace, and experience with training programs. SALIC is designed to provide these crucial data.

Initially three communities were selected for the survey: Chinatown/Echo Park, Koreatown/Westlake, and the Cambodian community in Long Beach. The goal was to have 100 completed interviews per community. During the survey, we expanded the number of interviews in the Filipinotown area of Westlake so we could have a larger number of Filipino respondents.

The sample was created in three steps. The first step was identifying the clusters of census tracts that are located in the three geographic areas and that have a population which is at least 15 percent Asian American according to the 1990 Census. These clusters were then divided into census blocks that were assigned a number by a random number generator, and at least a dozen blocks were randomly selected for surveying. Maps for the second step, and for guiding the interviewers during the survey, were constructed from the TIGER/Line files from the U.S. Census. The third step was to determine what proportion of the households should be interviewed so we can reach the desired number of completed surveys and maintain geographically diversity among the respondents. It was determined that every other household would be approach. Only Asian American households were interviewed.

Community leaders provided input during the initial development of the questionnaire, which was then reviewed by experts in the area of survey research. When possible, questions were worded in the form used by the census so our results could be compared to existing statistics. A pilot test was done to identify any potential problems, resulting in several modifications to the original questionnaire. The final instrument was translated into six languages (Chinese, Laotian, Vietnamese, Cambodian, Thai, and Korean), and each translation was reviewed for accuracy by a person other than the translators.

Interviews were conducted by undergraduate and graduate students from UCLA during the months of February and March of 1993. The interviewers participated in three four-hour long training sessions that covered issues of conduct and personal presentation, administering the questionnaire, handling difficult situations, and safety. Each interviewer was required to gain experience through role playing during the sessions. When possible, students who spoke an Asian language were assigned to communities according to their language abilities. The survey also used paid translators referred to the project by community-based organizations.

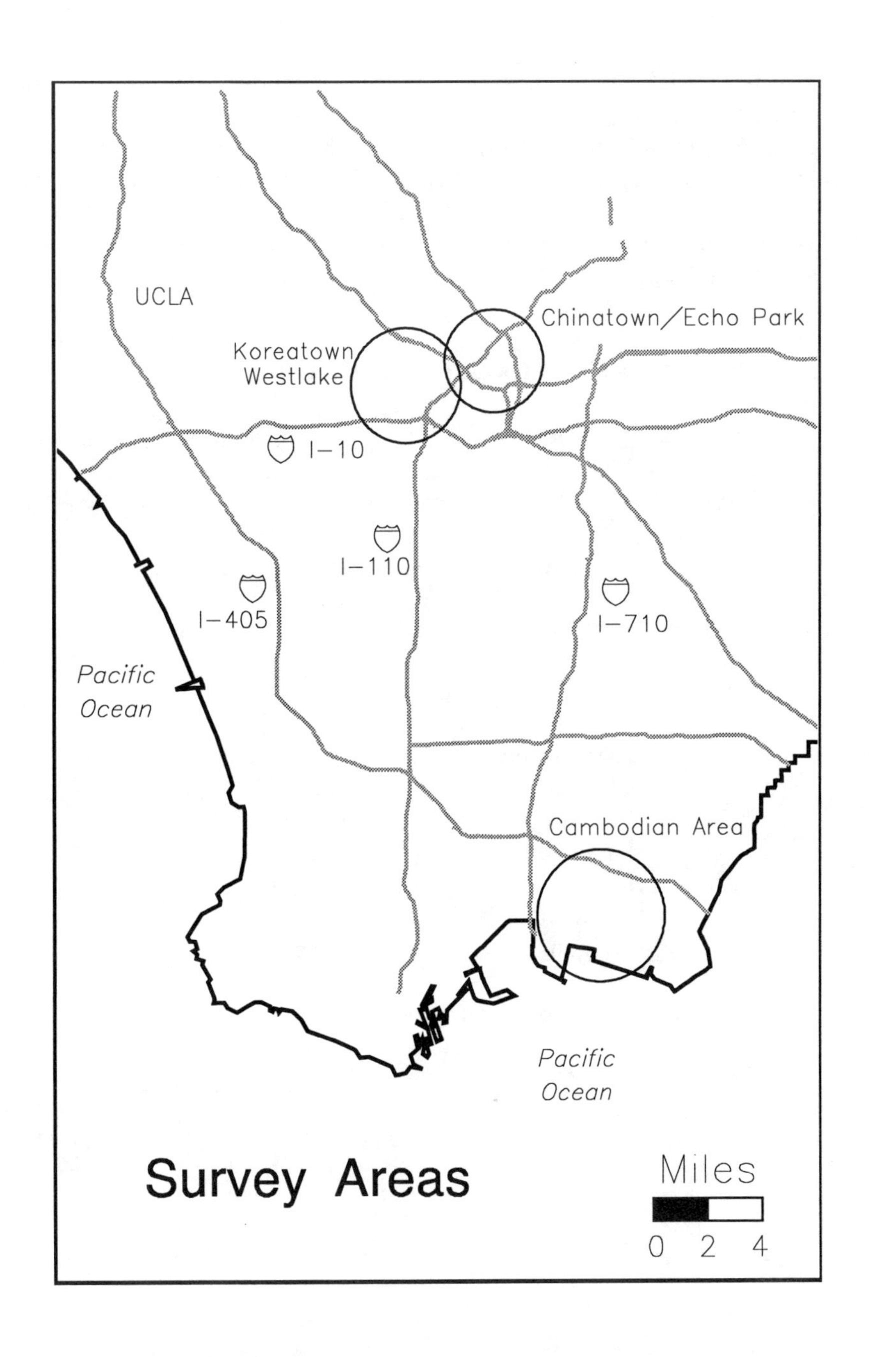
UCLA
Koreatown
Westlake
Chinatown/Echo Park
I-10
I-110
I-405
I-710
Pacific
Ocean
Cambodian Area
Pacific
Ocean
Survey Areas
Miles
0 2 4

UCLA ASIAN/PACIFIC ISLANDER COMMUNITY SURVEY

This is a UCLA survey of Asian and Pacific Islander communities. The survey contains questions about housing and employment. It will be used to help community organizations develop new programs and improve their services. Your answers will be kept strictly confidential and you name and address will not be used. If you are 16 or older, would you be willing to answer the following questions? This survey should take approximately 15 minutes to complete.

I. PRELIMINARY BACKGROUND INFORMATION:

1. ___Male ___Female

2. Are you the ___head of the household
   ___spouse of head of household
   ___other

3. What year were you born?________

4. What is your ethnic background?

___	Asian Indian	___	Cambodian
___	Chinese	___	Guamanian
___	Filipino	___	Native Hawaiian
___	Japanese	___	Laotian
___	Korean	___	Samoan
___	Vietnamese	___	Thai
___	Tongan	___	Other

5. Were you born in the United States? ___Yes ___No

   If **No**: In what country were you born?_________________

   What year did you move to the United States permanently?
____

   What was your occupation prior to coming to the United States?________

6. How well do you speak English? Please rank.

__Not at all __Not Well __Well __Very Well

7. How much school have you completed? (Include school in other countries)

___ Less than 9th grade
___ 9th to 12th grade, no diploma
___ High School Graduate, or equivalent
___ Some College, no degree
___ Associate Degree (AA)
___ Bachelor's Degree (BA or BS)
___ Graduate or Professional School

II. HOUSEHOLD:

8. Do you own or rent this residence? ___Own ___Rent

9. If rented, what is the monthly rent?________

If owned, what is the monthly mortgage?________

10. Do you have a living room?___

11. Not counting the living room, how many bedrooms does this apartment/house have?________

12. How many people live in this residence, including yourself?_____

13. Including yourself, what is the total monthly income of all members of this residence before taxes?__________

III. EMPLOYMENT:

14. Are you currently employed? (Not including self-employment)
___Yes ___No

15. How many separate jobs do you have?______

16. In a typical week, how many hours do you work?______

17. What is your occupation(s)?

___________ Job 1 ___________ Job 2 ___________ Job 3

18. What is the hourly wage of your current job(s)?

___________ Job 1 ___________ Job 2 ___________ Job 3

19. How many years have you been at your job(s)?

___________ Job 1 ___________ Job 2 ___________ Job 3

20. In a typical month, what is your take home income after taxes? (including tips and gratuities)

___________ Job 1 ___________ Job 2 ___________ Job 3

21. Is your work place within 5 miles of your home?

_____ Job 1 _____ Job 2 _____ Job 3

22. Does your employer pay for all or most of your medical insurance?

_____ Job 1 _____ Job 2 _____ Job 3

23. How did you find your current job(s)?

Job 1:____

Job 2:____

Job 3:____

24. What ethnicity is your supervisor?

___________ Job 1 ____________ Job 2 ______________ Job 3

25. If applicable, what is the ethnicity of the business owner where you work?

___________ Job 1 ______________ Job 2 ______________ Job 3

26. How many employees are there where you work?

________ Job 1 ________ Job 2 ________ Job 3

27. How many employees are the same ethnicity as you?

________ Job 1 ________ Job 2 ________ Job 3

28. Are you self-employed? ___Yes ___No

If No, skip to 34.

29. What type of business do you own?____________________

30. What is your personal net income per month from your business? ____________

31. Not including family members, how many employees work for you?_______

32. In a typical week, how many hours do you work?________

33. What year did you start your business?________

34. Last week, were you actively looking for a job?______

35. In your previous job, what was your occupation?______________

36. In your previous job, what was your hourly wage?_________

37. In your previous job, what was your typical monthly take home pay after taxes? (including tips and gratuities)?______________

38. Have you ever attended a job training program or taken classes to enhance your skills? ____Yes ___No

If yes, what institution or organization provided this program?

____

39. Have you ever taken English as a Second Language (ESL) classes?
___Yes ___No

If yes, what institution or organization provided this program?

____

Thank you for your cooperation. Would you be willing to participate in a more extensive interview? Your name and address will be kept strictly confidential. If yes, please fill in the information below.

Name_______________________________________

Address_____________________________________

Phone Number______________________

References

Aguilar, Armando (1993). Interview with Armando Aguilar, Chinatown Service Center conducted by Dennis Arguelles, July 26, 1993.

Akst, Daniel (1993). "Cruler Fates: Cambodians Find Slim Profit in Doughnuts," in *Los Angeles Times*, March 9, 1993.

Alaska, State of (1981). *Indochinese Refuge Resettlement.*

Amsun Associates (1977). *Socio-economic Analysis of Asian American Business Patterns.* A study prepared for the Office of Minority Business Enterprise, U.S. Department of Commerce. New Rochelle, New York, January.

Asian Americans and Pacific Islanders in Philanthropy (AAPIP) (1992). *Invisible and in Need: Philanthropic Giving to Asian Americans and Pacific Islanders.* San Francisco, CA: AAPIP.

Asian Pacific Planning Council (1992). Proposal for Funding for Liquor Store Business Conversion Program Development. Los Angeles, CA: APPCON.

Auster, Ellen and Howard Aldrich (1984). "Small Business Vulnerability, Ethnic Enclaves and Ethnic Enterprise," in *Ethnic Communities in Business*, eds., Robin Ward and Richard Jenkins, Cambridge, MA: Cambridge University Press.

Bailey, Thomas and Roger Waldinger (1991). "The Changing Ethnic/Racial Division of Labor," in *Dual City: Restructuring New York*, eds., John H. Mollenkopf and Manuel Castells, New York, NY: Russell Sage Foundation.

Bailey, Thomas and Roger Waldinger (1992). "Primary, Secondary, and Enclave Labor Markets: A Training Systems Approach," in *American Sociological Review*, Vol. 56, August, pp. 432-445.

Bassi, Laurie and Orley Ashenfelter (1986). "The Effect of Direct Job Creation and Training Programs on Low-Skilled Workers," in *Fighting Poverty: What Works and What Doesn't*, eds., Sheldon Danziger and Daniel Weinberg, Cambridge, MA: Harvard University Press.

Bates, Timothy (1989). "The Changing Nature of Minority Business: A Comparative Analysis of Asian, Nonminority, and Black-owned Businesses," in *The Review of Black Political Economy*, Vol. 18, Fall, pp. 25-42.

Bates, Timothy (1987). "Self-Employed Minorities: Traits and Trends," in *Social Science Quarterly*, Vol. 68, September, pp. 539-51.

Bates, Timothy (1985). "Entrepreneur Human Capital Endowments and Minority Business Viability," in *The Journal of Human Resources*, Vol. 20, Fall, pp. 540-554.

Berthoff, Rowland (1980). "Independence and Enterprise: Small Business in the American Dream," in *Small Business in American Life*, ed., Stuart W. Bruchey. New York, NY: Columbia University Press.

Blackford, Mansel G. (1991). *A History of Small Business in America*. New York, NY: Twayne Publishers.

Bonacich, Edna (1988). "The Social Costs of Immigrant Entrepreneurship," in *Amerasia Journal*, Vol. 14, No. 1, pp. 119-128.

Bonacich, Edna (1987). "Making it in America: A Social Evaluation of the Ethics of Immigrant Entrepreneurship," in *Sociological Perspectives*, Vol. 30, No.4, October, pp. 446-466.

Boyd, Robert L. (1991). "Inequality in the Earnings of Self-Employed African and Asian Americans," in *Sociological Perspectives*, Vol. 34, No. 4, pp. 447-472.

Bratt, Rachel G. (1989). *Rebuilding a Low Income Housing Policy*. Philadelphia, PA: Temple University Press.

Brity, William P. (1972). *Puzzles in the Demographic and Economic Behavior of Rural Southeast Asians: An Economic View*. Santa Monica, CA: The Rand Corporation.

Brock, William A. and David S. Evans (1986). *The Economics of Small Businesses: Their Role and Regulations in the U.S. Economy*, New York, NY: Holmes and Meier.

Brock, William A. and David S. Evans (1989). "Small Business Economics," in *Small Business Economics I*, pp. 7-20.

Bruchey, Stuart W., ed. (1980). *Small Business in American Life*. New York, NY: Columbia University Press.

California, State of (1985). Employment Development Department, Data and Research Division. *Costs to the Unemployment Fund of Training and Retraining Programs*. Sacramento, CA.

California, State of (1992). Employment Development Department, Labor Market Information Division. *Annual Planning Information: Los Angeles-Long Beach*. Sacramento, CA.

California, State of (1987). Office of the Legislative Analyst. *A Review of the Job Training Partnership Act Program In California*. Sacramento, CA.

California, State of (1991). Senate Committee on Local Government. "Use-It-Or-Lose-It: A Legislative Review of Redevelopment Agencies' Housing Program. A Summary Report from the Interim Hearing of the Senate Committee on Local Government." Sacramento, CA, December 17, 1991.

California, State of (1991). Tax Credit Allocation Committee. "1990 Annual Report: Report on the Allocation of Federal and State Low Income Housing Tax Credits in California." April 1, 1991.

California, State of (1992). Tax Credit Allocation Committee. "1991 Annual Report: Report on the Allocation of Federal and State Low Income Housing Tax Credits in California." April 1, 1992.

California, State of (1981). *Horizon: An Overview of Vocational Education and Employment Training Services for Limited-English Proficient Persons in California.*

California, State of (1990). *California Statewide Housing Plan Update.* October.

California, State of (1985). *California Labor Laws: Rights for all Workers.* California: Industrial Relations.

California, State of (1989). Division of Labor Standards Enforcement. "Official Notice: Industrial Welfare Commission Order No. 1-89, Regulating Wages, Hours, and Working Conditions in the Manufacturing Industry." *Title 8: California, Code of Regulations.*

California, State of (1990). Division of Labor Standards Enforcement. "Laws Relating to Payment of Wages." *Title 8: California, Code of Regualtions.*

Capgart, Jim (1993). Interview with Jim Capgart, U.S. Small Business Administration, conducted by Tarry Hum, March 12, 1993.

Center for Community Change (1985). *Organizing for Neighborhood Development,* Washington D.C.: CCC Publications.

Chang, Yusa (1993). Interview with Yusa Chang, Deputy Director of Pacific Asian Consortium in Employment, conducted by Winnie Louie on April 21, 1993.

Chavez, Bonnie (1992). "Limited Gains with GAIN." Student Paper. UCLA Graduate School of Architecture and Urban Planning.

Ching, Deborah (1993). Interview with Deborah Ching, President of Asian Pacific Planning Council, conducted by Erich Nakano on April 9, 1993.

Ching, Deborah (1993). Interview with Deborah Ching, Executive Director, Chinatown Service Center, conducted by Dennis Arguelles, May 1993.

Chhim, Him (1992). Interview with Him Chhim, Executive Director, Cambodian Association of America conducted by Winnie Louie, June 1, 1992.

Chun, Jennifer (1993). Interview with Jennifer Chun, Korean Youth and Community Center, conducted by Ricky Ramos, 1993.

Chun, Jennifer (1993). Interview with Jennifer Chun, Korean Youth and Community Center, conducted by Dennis Arguelles, July 22, 1993.

Chung, Kimberly (1993). Interview with Kimberly Chung, Pacific ACE, Interview conducted by Ricky Ramos, 1993.

City of Los Angeles (1992). Community Development Department. Informational brochure on the Industrial and Commerical Development Division.

City of Los Angeles (1993). Community Development Department. Los Angeles Revitalization Zone Fact Sheet (1992-3).

City of Los Angeles (1992). Community Redevelopment Agency. Chinatown Redevelopment Project brochure.

City of Los Angeles (1992). Housing Authority. 1992 Annual Report.

City of Los Angeles (1991). Housing Preservation and Production Department. *Comprehensive Housing Affordability Strategy* (CHAS). November 1991.

City of Los Angeles (1992). Housing Preservation and Production Department. *Comprehensive Housing Affordability Strategy, Fiscal Years 1992 Through 1996.*

City of Los Angeles (1993). Housing Preservation and Production Department. *Comprehensive Housing Affordability Strategy (CHAS): Annual Plan Fiscal Year 1993.* February 1993.

Clark, David. Interview with David Clark, Assistant Director, Housing Assisted Payments Program (Section 8), conducted by Susan Castro, January 28, 1993.

Clavel, Pierre and Wim Wiewel, eds. (1991). *Harold Washington and the Neighborhoods: Progressive City Government in Chicago, 1983-1987*, New Brunswick, NJ: Rutgers University Press.

Cohen, Rick (1992). "Getting Your Piece of the New Federal Home Funds," in *Shelterforce*, May/June.

County of Los Angeles (1992). Department of Social Services, Statistical Services. "Annual Recipient Report on AFDC, Social Services, Nonassistance Food Stamps, and RCA Ethnic Origin and Primary Language," April 1992.

Desbarats, Jacqueline (1979). "Thai Migration to Los Angeles," in *Geographical Review*, Vol. 69, pp. 302-318.

Doherty, Jake (1993). "Westlake, Affordable Housing Projects Lined Up," in *Los Angeles Times*, City Times section, Sunday, May 16, 1993, p. 9.

Donahue, John (1989). *Shortchanging the Workforce: The Job Training Partnership Act and the Overselling of Privatized Training.* Washington D.C.: Economic Policy Institute.

duRivage, Virgina L. (1992). "New Policies for the Part-Time and Contingent Workforce," in *New Policies for the Part-Time and Contingent Workforce,* ed., Virginia duRivage, London, England: M.E. Sharpe, Inc.

Ehrbar, Al (1993). "Proposed Tax Incentives for Businesses May Have Little Impact, Analysts Say," in *Wall Street Journal,* March 11, 1993.

Ellwood, David T. (1988). *Poor Support: Poverty in the American Family.* New York, NY: Basic Books.

Friedlander, Daniel, James Riccio, and Stephen Freedman (1993). "GAIN: Two-Year Impacts in Six Counties," Manpower Demonstration Research Corporation, May.

Fritz, Sara (1993). "White House Message: The Uninsured Are Just Like Us," in *Los Angeles Times,* May 23.

Gardner, J.M., and D.E. Herz (1992). "Working and Poor in 1990," in *Monthly Labor Review,* December, Vol. 115, No. 12, pp. 20-28.

Goldfield, Michael (1989). *The Decline of Organized Labor in the United States.* Chicago, IL: The University of Chicago Press.

Goldsmith, William and Edward Blakely (1992). *Separate Societies: Poverty and Inequality in U.S. Cities.* Philadelphia, PA: Temple University Press.

Greenstein, Robert and Scott Barancik (1990). *Drifting Apart: New Findings on Growing Income Disparities between the Rich, the Poor and the Middle Class.* Washington D.C.: Center on Budget and Policy Priorities.

Ha, Minh (1993). Interview with Minh Ha, Department of Public Social Services, Headquarters of the GAIN program, conducted by Susan Castro, May 3, 1993.

Harrington, Howard and Christopher Cheleden (1991). "An Analysis of Los Angeles At-Risk HUD Projects and Critique of the 'Low Income Housing Preservation and Resident Homeownership Act of 1990,' a client project for the UCLA Graduate School of Architecture and Urban Planning, June 14, 1991.

Harrison, Bennett and Barry Bluestone (1988). *The Great U-Turn: Corporate Restructuring and the Polarizing of America.* New York, NY: Basic Books.

Hasenfeld, Yeheske (1991). "The Implementation of GAIN in Los Angeles County: 1988-1990." Unpublished Paper. UCLA School of Social Welfare, Center for Child and Family Policy Studies. December.

Hernandez, Sandra (1993). Interview with Sandra Hernandez, United Cambodian Center, conducted by Ricky Ramos, 1993.

Hill, Joanna (1993). Interview with Ms. Joanna Hill, Valley Economic Development Corporation conducted by Chanchanit Hirunpidok, June 7, 1993.

Hing, Bill Ong (1993). "Making and Remaking Asian Pacific America: Immigration Policy," in *The State of Asian Pacific America: Policy Issues to the Year 2020*, ed., Leadership Education for Asian Pacifics (LEAP), Los Angeles, CA: LEAP and UCLA Asian American Studies Center, pp. 127-140.

Hirunpidok, Chanchanit (1992). "The Community Reinvestment Act as a Tool for Low Income Housing Development." Student Paper. UCLA Graduate School of Architecture and Urban Planning, June 8, 1992.

Hoffman, Saul D. (1990). *The Earned Income Tax Credit: Anti-Poverty Effectiveness and Labor Market Effects*. Michigan: W. E. Upjohn Institute for Employment Research.

Hoffman, Wayne L. (1978). *The Earned Income Tax Credit: Welfare Reform or Tax Relief? An Analysis of Alternative Proposals*. Washington D.C.: The Urban Institute.

Hum, Tarry and Paul Ong (1992). "Asian Pacific Americans in Los Angeles County: Demographic Trends and Public Policy Implications," Monograph Draft. October.

ICF Incorporated (1992). "Welcome Home For Nonprofits, An Introduction To The HOME Program." November 9, 1992.

Joe, Glenda K. (1992). "Asian American Merchants Handbook." Houston, Texas: Asian Community Support Services Center.

Joe, Tom and Timothy Eckels (1981). "Enterprise Development as an Employment Strategy for Welfare Recipients," in Robert Friedman and William Schweke, eds., *Expanding the Opportunity to Produce: Revitalizing the American Economy Through New Enterprise Development*. Washington D.C.: The Corporation for Enterprise Development.

Judd, Richard J., William T. Greenwood, and Fred W. Becker, eds. (1988). *Small Business in a Regulated Economy: Issues and Policy Implications*. Westport, CT: Quorum Books.

June, Rodney (1993). Interview with Rodney June, Management Assistant for HPPD's Budget Development/Administrative Services, conducted by Bruce Chow, January 28, 1993.

Katz, Michael B. (1986). *In the Shadow of the Poor House: A Social History of Welfare in America*. New York, NY: Basic Books.

Kennedy, Marie (1986). "If Free Enterprise Zones Don't Work, Why All the Controversy?" Unpublished Paper. William M. Tucker Institute for the Study of Black Culture, University of Massachusetts at Boston.

Khalid, Somsri Dr., and Lan Nguyen, Megan Merthold, Sophet Sayakhot, Ranomati Saing and Hoa Ly (1992). Interview with Indochinese Refugee Counseling Center conducted by Erich Nakano, July 9, 1992.

Kim, Helen (1993). Interview with Helen Kim, Project Manager for Korean Youth and Community Center conducted by Bruce Chow, March, 16, 1993.

Kim, Kwang Chung, Won Moo Hurh, and Marilyn Fernandez (1989). "Intra-Group Differences in Business Participation: Three Asian Immigrant Groups," in *International Migration Review*, Vol. 23, No. 1, pp. 73-95.

Kim, Richard, Kane Nakamura, Gisele Fong, Ron Cabarloc, Barbara Jung and Lee Sung (1992). "A Preliminary Investigation Asian Immigrant Women Garment Workers in Los Angeles," in *Amerasia Journal*, Vol. 18, No. 1.

Kirkpatrick, David H., Mary Ann Dillon and Susan Bloch (1987). "Developments in Nonprofit Production of Low Income Housing," in *Clearinghouse Review*. January 1987, p. 1234.

Kotkin, Joel (1993). *Tribes: How Race, Religion, and Family Determine Success in the New Global Economy*. New York, NY: Random House.

Kwoh, Stewart (1993). "Empowering Our Communities: Political Policy", in *The State of Asian/Pacific America: Policy Issues to the Year 2020*, eds., LEAP and UCLA Asian American Studies Center, p. 194.

Kwong, Peter (1987). *The New Chinatown*. New York, NY: Hill and Wang.

Labor/Community Strategy Center (1993). *Reconstructing Los Angeles From the Bottom Up*. Los Angeles, CA.

Lang, Smith (1993). Interview with Smith Lang, United Cambodian Center, conducted by Ricky Ramos, 1993.

Lazere, Edward B, Paul A. Leonard, Cushing N. Dolbeare, and Barry Zigas (1991). "A Place to Call Home: The Low Income Housing Crisis Continues," Washington D.C.: Center on Budget and Policy Priorities. December 1991.

Le, Ngoan (1993). "The Case of the Southeast Asian Refugees: Policy for a Community "At-Risk," from *The State of Asian Pacific America: Policy Issues to the Year 2020*, ed., Leadership Education for Asian Pacifics (LEAP), Los Angeles, CA: LEAP and UCLA Asian American Studies Center.

LEAP Asian Pacific American Public Policy Institute and the UCLA Asian American Studies Center (1993). *The State of Asian Pacific America: Policy Issues to the Year 2020*. Los Angeles, CA: LEAP and UCLA Asian American Studies Center.

Lee, Michael (1993). Interview with Mr. Michael Lee, Division Director, US Small Business Administration conducted by Tarry Hum, March 12, 1993.

Levitan, Sar A. and Frank Gallo (1987). "The Targeted Jobs Tax Credit: An Uncertain and Unfinished Experiment," in *Labor Law Journal*, Vol. 38, No. 20, pp. 641-649.

Levitan, Sar A. and Frank Gallo (1992). *Spending to Save: Expanding Employment Opportunties*. Washington, D.C.: Center for Social Policy Studies, George Washington University.

Levitan, Sar A. and Richard S. Belous (1979). *More than Subsistence: Minimum Wages for the Working Poor*. Baltimore, MD: The Johns Hopkins University Press.

Light, Ivan (1972). *Ethnic Enterprise in America: Business and Welfare Among Chinese, Japanese, and Blacks*. Berkeley, CA: University of California Press.

Light, Ivan and Edna Bonacich (1988). *Immigrant Entrepreneurs: Koreans in Los Angeles*, 1965-1982. Berkeley, CA: University of California Press.

Little Tokyo Community Development Advisory Committee Membership Roster, November 1991.

Luu, Huy Quoc (1993). Interview with anonymous conducted by Huy Quoc Luu, March 9, 1993.

Mar, Don (1991). "Another Look at the Enclave Economy Thesis: Chinese Immigrants in the Ethnic Labor Market," in *Amerasia Journal*, Vol. 17, No. 3, pp. 28-42.

Mason, Sarah R. (1986). *Training Southeast Asian Refugee Women for Employment: Public Policies and Community Programs*, 1975-85. Minnesota: University of Minnesota.

Massey, Doreen (1982). "Enterprise Zones: Some Concerns. A Preliminary Position Paper." Unpublished Paper. Boston, MA: Massachusetts Community Action.

Maxted, Julia and Abebe Zegeye (1991). "Race, Class and Polarization in Los Angeles," in *Exploitation and Exclusion*, eds., A. Zegeye, L. Harris and J. Maxted, London: Hans Zell Publisher.

May, Lee (1987). "Asians Looking to Broaden Horizons: Immigrants Prosper but Hope to Venture Outside the 'Business Ghetto'," in *Los Angeles Times*, February 2.

Medrano, Michael A. (1993). Interview with Michael Medrano, California State of Industrial Relations, Division of Labor Standards Enforcement, conducted by Susan Castro in Los Angeles, CA, May 1993.

Mike and Phil (1993). Interview with Mike and Phil, Inspectors at Cal/OSHA, Occupational Safety and Health Administration, conducted by Susan Castro in Los Angeles, CA, on May 3, 1993.

Min, Pyong Gap (1984). "From White Collar Occupations to Small Business: Korean Immigrants Occupational Adjustments," in *The Sociological Quarterly*, Vol. 25, Summer, pp. 333-352.

Min, Pyong Gap (1984). "A Structural Analysis of Korean Business in the United States," in *Ethnic Groups*, Vol. 6, pp. 1-25.

Min, Pyong Gap (1986). "Filipino and Korean Immigrants in Small Business: A Comparative Analysis," in *Amerasia Journal*, Vol. 13 No. 1, pp. 53-71.

Mokry, Benjamin W. (1988). *Entrepreneurship and Public Policy.* New York, NY: Quorum Books.

Nakamura, Fred (1992). Interview with Fred Nakamura, Legal Aid Foundation of Los Angeles, conducted by Erich Nakano on November 17, 1992 and December 3, 1992.

National Coalition for the Homeless (1991). "The Closing Door: Economic Causes of Homelessness," *Practicing Law Institute*, Vol. 428, January 22, 1991, p. 799.

National Congress for Community Economic Development (NCCED) (1991). *Changing the Odds.* Washington D.C.: NCCED.

National Low Income Housing Preservation Commission (1988). "Preventing the Disappearance of Low Income Housing," Washington D.C.

Nee, Victor and Jimy Sanders (1987). "On Testing the Enclave-Economy Hypothesis" in *American Sociological Review*, Vol. 52, December, pp. 771-773.

Ng, Johnson (1993). Interview with Johnson Ng, Chinatown Service Center conducted by Ricky Ramos.

North, David (1992). *An Evaluation of the Planned Secondary Resettlement Program.* Washington: CZA, Inc.

Ong, Paul (1984). "Chinatown Unemployment and Ethnic Labor Markets," in *Amerasia Journal*, Vol. 11, No. 1.

Ong, Paul and Tania Azores (1993). "Asian Immigrants in Los Angeles: Diversity and Divisions" in *Struggles For A Place: New Asian Immigrants in Los Angeles* (Pending Publication).

Ong, Paul and Suzanne J. Hee (1993). "Twenty Million in 2020," in The *State of Asian Pacific America*, ed., Leadership Education for Asian Pacifics (LEAP), Los Angeles: LEAP and UCLA Asian American Studies Center, pp. 11-24.

Pastor, Manuel, et. al. (1990). *Economic Development: The New Majority in Los Angeles*, Los Angeles, CA: The New Majority Organizing Committee.

Pilland, William E. (1986). *Vocational Education and Employment Training in California.* Illinois: Center for Higher Education, Illinois State University

Piore, Michael J. (1990). "The Re-emergence of Small Enterprises: United States of America," in *The Re-emergence of Small Enterprises: Industrial Restructuring in Industrialized Countries*. eds., Werner Sengenberger, Gary W. Loveman, and Michael J. Piore. Geneva: International Institute for Labour Studies.

Pok, Than (1992). Interview with Than Pok, Executive Director, United Cambodian Community conducted by Dennis Arguelles, Chancee Hirunpidok, Susan Castro, Bruce Chow, and Winnie Louie, June 5, 1992.

Portes, Alejandro and Leif Jensen (1987). "What's an Ethnic Enclave? The Case for Conceptual Clarity," in *American Sociological Review*, Vol. 52, December, pp. 768-771.

Portes, Alejandro and Robert L. Bach (1985). *Latin Journey: Cuban and Mexican Immigrants in the United States*. Berkeley, CA: University of California Press.

Racaniello, Frank, A. (1991). "Extending the Low Income Housing Tax Credit," in *Rutgers University Law Journal*, Spring, Vol. 22, p. 753.

Razin, Eran (1989). "Entrepreneurship Among Foreign Immigrants in the Los Angeles and San Francisco Metropolitan Regions," in *Urban Geography*, Vol. 9, No. 3, pp. 283-301.

Rezabek, Dale and Christine Saul (1986). *Preparing Californians To Work: A Local Perspective on JTPA and Education Coordination*. California State Council on Vocational Education, October.

Romero, Fred and Judith Gonzales (1989). *Falling Through The Cracks: Hispanic Underrepresentation in the Job Training Partnership Act*. Washington D.C.: Office of Research Advocacy and Legislation.

Rubin, Alissa (1993). "Reinvention of Health Care is Key to Clinton Overhaul." *Congressional Quarterly*, 51, March 13, 1993, pp. 595-600.

Rudman, Cary and Clematee Meredith, Jr. (1990). *Ready Or Not, Here We Come: Training California's Emerging Workforce*. Sacramento, CA: Assembly Office of Research.

Sanders, Jimy and Victor Nee (1987). "Limits of Ethnic Solidarity in the Enclave Economy," in *American Sociological Review*, Vol. 52, December, pp. 745-767.

Sanders, Jo (1988). *Staying Poor: How The Job Training Partnership Act Fails Women*. Metuchen: Scarecrow Press.

Schindler, Elizabeth (1992). "Planning for Small Business Assistance in Los Angeles." Masters Thesis, UCLA Urban Planning Program.

Schnidman, Frank (1991). "Affordable Housing: The Government Responses," American Law Institute-American Bar Association. Q203, January 24, 1991, p. 283.

Sengupta, Somini (1993). "A Neighborly Approach to Saving Low Income Housing," in *Los Angeles Times*, Metro Section, April 25, 1993, p. 1.

Shiver, Jube Jr. (1992). "Through the Roof," in *Los Angeles Times*, Business section, June 21, 1992, pp. D1 - D7.

Shogren, Elizabeth (1993). "Tax Credit Aims to Lift Families Out of Poverty," in *Los Angeles Times*, February 20, 1993.

Silas, Curtis (1993). Interview with Curtis Silas, Pacific Asian Consortium on Employment, conducted by Ricky Ramos, 1993.

Skocpol, Theda (1991). "Targeting Within Universalism: Politically Viable Policies to Combat Poverty in the United States," in *The Urban Underclass*, eds., Christopher Jencks and Paul E. Peterson, Washington, D.C.: Brookings Institution.

Solomon, Steven (1986). *Small Business USA: The Role of Small Companies in Sparking America's Economic Transformation*. New York, NY: Crown Publishers, Inc.

Soja, Edward W. (1987). "Economic Restructuring and the Internationalization of the Los Angeles Region," in *The Capitalist City*, eds., M.P. Smith and J.R. Feagin, New York, NY: B. Blackwell.

Stolarik, Mark M. and Murray Friedman, eds (1986). *Making it in America: The Role of Ethnicity in Business Enterprise, Education, and Work Choices*. London: Associated University Press.

Stone, Michael E. (1990). "One-Third of a Nation: A New Look at Housing Affordability in America." Booklet. Washington D.C.: Economic Policy Institute.

Stout, Hilary (1993). "Health-Care Experts Devising Clinton Plan Face Sticky Questions," in *Wall Street Journal*, March 11, 1993.

Sugino, Lisa (1993). Interview with Lisa Sugino, Program Coordinator, Little Tokyo Service Center Housing Program, conducted by Erich Nakano, May 4, 1993.

Survey of Asian Low-Income Communities (SALIC) (1993). Developed and conducted by Dennis Arguelles, Susan Castro, Bruce Chow, Chanchanit Hirunpidok, Winnie Louie, Erich Nakano, and Ricky Ramos for UCLA Urban Planning Program Comprehensive Project.

Sy, Albert (1993). Interview with Albert Sy, Pacific Asian Consortium in Employment, conducted by Dennis Arguelles, July 23, 1993.

Tilly, Chris (1992). "Short Hours, Short of Part-Time Employment," in *New Policies for the Part-Time and Contingent Workforce*, ed. Virgina duRivage, London, England: M.E. Sharpe, Inc.

Toji, Dean S. and James H. Johnson (1992). "Asian and Pacific Islander American Poverty: The Working Poor and the Jobless Poor," in *Amerasia Journal*, Vol. 18, No. 1.

Toy, Don (1993). Interview with Don Toy, Vice Chair of Chinatown Community Advisory Committee (CCAC), conducted by Winnie Louie on March 19, 1993.

Tuione, Siona (1992). Interview with Siona Tuione, Director of Tongan Community Service Center conducted by Winnie Louie and Erich Nakano on May 29, 1992 in Gardena, CA.

Ulman, Lloyd (1974). "The Uses and Limits of Manpower Policy," in *The Great Society*, eds., Eli Ginzber and Robert M. Solow, New York, NY: Basic Books.

United States. Bureau of the Census. 1990 PUMS, Los Angeles County data.

United States. Bureau of the Census. 1990 STF3A, Los Angeles County data.

United States. Bureau of the Census. 1972, 1977, 1987 Survey of Minority-Owned Businesses -- Asian Americans, American Indians, and Others. Washington, D.C.

United States. Committee on Education and Labor (1988). "Section-by-Section Analysis of Job Training Partnership Act." Washington, D.C.: U.S. Government Printing Office.

United States. General Accounting Office (1991). "Targeted Jobs Tax Credit: Employer Actions to Recruit, Hire, and Retain Eligible Workers Vary," Washington, D.C.: GAO.

United States. General Accounting Office (1991). "Job Training Partnership Act: Racial and Gender Disparities in Services," Washington, D.C.: GAO.

United States. General Accounting Office (1993). "The Job Training Partnership Act: Potential for Program Improvements But National Job Training Strategy Needed," Washington, D.C.: GAO.

United States Congress. House of Representatives. 102nd Session. Basic Laws on Housing and Community Development. September 30, 1991.

United States Congress. House of Representatives, Committee on Ways and Means. "Overview of Entitlement Programs; 1990 Green Book; Background Material and Data on Programs Within the Jurisdiction of the Committee on Ways and Means." June 1990.

United States Congress. Joint Committee on Taxation. "Estimates of Federal Tax Expenditures for Fiscal Year 1993-1997." April 24, 1992.

United States Senate. 139 Congressional Record S3549, March 24, 1993.

United States Small Business Administration (1992). *Today's SBA Means Business.*

United States Subcommittee on Employment and Productivity (1984). "Preliminary Oversight on the Job Training Partnership Act." Washington, D.C.: US Government Printing Office.

United States Subcommittee on Employment and Productivity (1982). "Compilation of Selected Federal Legislation Relating to Job Training." Washington, D.C.: U.S. Government Printing Office.

Van Auken, Philip M. and R. Duane Ireland (1988). "Divergent Perspectives on Social Responsibility: Big Business versus Small," in Richard J. Judd, William T. Greenwood and Fred W. Becker, eds., *Small Business in a Regulated Economy: Issues and Policy Implications.* New York, NY: Quorum Books.

Waldinger, Roger, Robin Ward and Howard Aldrich (1985). "Ethnic Business and Occupational Mobility in Advanced Societies," in *Sociology*, Vol. 19, No. 4., pp. 586-597.

Waldinger, Roger (1989). "Structural Opportunity or Ethnic Advantage? Immigrant Business Development in New York," in *International Migration Review*, Vol. 23, No. 1, pp. 48-72.

Watanabe, Teresa and Soon Neo Lim (1990). "Feeling Isolated, Asian Entrepreneurs Want to Go Mainstream," in *Los Angeles Times*, August 6 1990.

Watts, Tim J. (1991). *Refugee Law in the United States Since the Refugee Act of 1980: A Bibliography.* Indiana: Valparaiso University.

Wing, Linda (1993). Interview with Linda Wing, Coordinator of Urban Superintendents Program, Graduate School of Education, Harvard University, conducted by Paul Ong, July 16, 1993.

Wong, Kent (1993). Interview with Kent Wong, Director, UCLA's Center for Labor Education and Research conducted by Paul Ong, July 23, 1993.

Wong, Vicky (1993). Interview with Vicky Wong, Chinatown Service Center, conducted by Ricky Ramos, 1993.

Yates, Larry (1990). "Low Income Housing In America: An Introduction." Booklet. Washington D.C.: Low Income Housing Information Service.

Zhou, Min and John R. Logan (1991). "Returns on Human Capital in Ethnic Enclaves: New York City's Chinatown," in *American Sociological Review*, Vol. 54, pp. 809-820.

About the Authors

Dennis Arguelles is currently a community planner for the Coalition of Neighborhood Developers. He is active with Asian Pacific Americans for a New Los Angeles (APANLA) and is working to build the community development capacity of Search to Involve Pilipino Americans, Inc., a nonprofit social service agency.

Susan Castro is continuing her work on urban issues such as housing, overcrowding and neighborhood revitalization as a Coro Fellow. She has worked at various local planning and community development agencies and was past chair of UCLA's Minority Association of Planners and Architects (MAPA).

Bruce Chow has worked for the Community Development Department of the City of San Fernando and is currently employed by Kaku Associates, Inc., where he is involved with transportation planning issues. He plans to continue his community service work by linking housing, transportation and land use policies.

Chanchanit (Chancee) Hirunpidok is currently a community planner for the Coalition of Neighborhood Developers. Her experience includes working for various local, state and federal legislative offices. She is the Executive Director of the American-Thai Education and Research Institute, a nonprofit agency serving the rapidly growing Thai community in Los Angeles.

Tarry Hum is working on her Ph.D. at the UCLA Graduate School of Architecture and Urban Planning. Her research interests include racial economic inequality and urban labor markets. Prior to relocating to Los Angeles, she was active in community planning and development work in Boston's Chinatown.

Winnie Louie is completing her concurrent degree program in urban planning and law. She worked for several years in the social services field coordinating employment training services for recent Chinese and other low-income immigrants, and is exploring options in utilizing her training and experience in both urban planning and law to improve the status of low-income individuals.

Erich Nakano is a Project Manager for the Little Tokyo Service Center and chairs the Liquor Store Task Force and the Housing and Economic Development Committee of the Asian Pacific Planning Council (APPCON). He is working on capacity-building initiatives and the coordination of community development activities in the Asian Pacific community.

Paul Ong is an associate professor at the UCLA Graduate School of Architecture and Urban Planning, and has authored and co-authored numerous articles on Asian Americans and issues of racial inequalities.

Ricky Ramos has worked for the Community Development Department of City of Los Angeles and other local agencies where he has been involved with various economic development projects. He is interested in land use planning and urban design and intends to pursue them by working in the public sector.